# Travel Writing 2.0

*Earning money from your travels in the new media landscape*

## By Tim Leffel

Printed in the United States of America.

Splinter Press
2010

# Dedication

To the next batch of brilliant travel writers, creative bloggers, and inventive entrepreneurs with something original to say.

# Contents

# Introduction

I woke up at 6:00 am, rolling out from under the covers of a cheap bed, immediately throwing some clothes on because the room was drafty. I set to work getting a blog entry posted and answering e-mails before my research day started. After two hours of writing and taking care of some business, the streets of central Mexico City became my research project, starting with breakfast at a historic café on my list. After taking notes from the meal and menu, an hour of walking followed to check the prices and décor or other breakfast options.

After that it was walk-throughs of two hotels to see rooms and public areas and popping by two art galleries to check the hours. I met a local author for lunch to get the inside scoop from a resident, then hit four more hotels in the afternoon, with another parade of rooms, restaurants, and lobbies. I did a walk-by of five restaurants along the way, jotting down enough notes to update the listings. Two were closed, so they'd have to be replaced with something else.

After grabbing a quick dinner at a well-known taco stand I needed to write about, I returned to my room at 8:00 pm, 12 hours after I had left. Opening my laptop back up, there were four e-mails that needed immediate attention before I could call it a day. The rest would have to wait. An hour later I showered and crawled into bed.

The second day was a repeat, same hours, different stops. For six more days after that I followed varying versions of this schedule, finally slowing down one day to tour the pyramids of Teotihuacán and the Basilica de Guadalupe. The last day in the city was dedicated to two things: visiting the Archeological Museum and writing in my room.

I got half-crushed in a subway car, went through a full bottle of tequila, and gained five pounds from all the street food I ate. In the end I worked eight days straight without a break, for assignments that added up to roughly $1,200 after expenses. I flew home on a crowded economy flight and was met by a wife who couldn't wait to tell me all the mom-at-home-alone crap she had to deal with while I was "having fun on my trip to Mexico."

Am I a masochist?

No, I am a travel writer.

Getting paid to do what you love—a dream job, right? I could make you salivate from the start with all kinds of dreamy weeks I have experienced while getting paid to explore exotic locations around the world. I'd promise you lots of wonderful perks and a life of leisure. I'd open with all the ways I'm going to give you the keys to the kingdom, promising that in 90 days you'd be exploring Tahiti with a nice magazine feature assignment that will earn you a few thousand dollars.

But that's not fair. It's not fair because there's a long journey involved before any of that happens. Sure the perks are great, but only after you reach a point where you are influential enough to deserve them.

Many travel writing seminars and retreats mostly focus on the glamorous side of the business because that's what brings in the students and the bucks. Heck, it's even what most books about travel writing do. They lay it all out like a display of pastries at a French bakery, with lots of exclamation points in their come-on copy. Get paid to travel! Free trips! Luxury suites at beach resorts! Live your life like a permanent vacation!

You can find similar ads for seminars on how to break into modeling, how to break into acting, or how to make it as a songwriter. It's all about the payoff, with very little about the tough odds you face to get there—or the vast majority of aspirants who never make it at all.

You deserve to hear the real story instead.

Here you'll get the truth from real travel writers and editors. With their help, you'll learn how to make actual money and enjoy yourself, with eyes wide open on what to expect along the way.

I don't think any of the writers included in this book would classify their work as anything close to being a "permanent vacation." For a guidebook writer, it's more like "permanently working my butt off while everyone around me is on vacation." Sure, the job is often a lot of fun, so I will touch on the things I love about my work. But it's unfair to tout the positives without detailing the corresponding trade-offs—especially the financial ones.

Thomas Kohnstamm laid it out well in the intro of his controversial book *Do Travel Writer's Go to Hell?* He said, "I imagine that the difference between traveling and professional travel writing is the difference between having sex and working in pornography. While both are still probably fun, being a professional brings many levels of complication to your original interest and will eventually consume your personal life."

Perhaps more important than the reality check, this is a book about the here and now, not about what used to be. The elements of the book itself are all meant to illustrate that point. The title (*Travel Writing 2.0*) refers directly to the new age of self-directed writing we have already entered. The means of production I am using (e-books and print-on-demand) reflect the reality that the publishing system of the last century is not serving us well in the new one. The methods of gathering data and advice for this book are also appropriate to the participatory climate the internet has created, rather than the top-down declaration-making that has existed since the dawn of the printing press.

The chapters to follow will outline the ways to make money as a travel writer in the new environment, with the pros and cons of each. It's clearer every month that the old highway is cracking in the heat behind us, so most of what was written in earlier travel writing books is quickly becoming fossilized. Following the traditional road of endless query letters, slowly breaking into print magazines, and making good money writing guidebooks doesn't cut it anymore for the new writers arriving on the scene—or even some that have been doing it for ages. Here you'll get advice for succeeding in a media landscape turned upside down.

Most travel writing books you pick up spend most of their pages on the craft itself and the earnings part is treated as an afterthought. I think that's backwards. There are already a thousand other books out there on how to be a good writer. They'll instruct you on how to be observant, avoid clichés, construct a narrative, define characters through action, write tight sentences, and all the other skills that are 90% the same whether you are writing about sports, business, food, politics, or travel. Go to your local library and you'll probably see shelves and shelves filled with these books. Check out a few and heed their advice. Read four or five of them to recognize the common threads. I have yet to meet a writer who thinks she is so skilled and talented that nothing she has written can be improved. We spend our whole lives learning and improving.

Since that "how to write well" job has already been done well by others over the course of decades, I'm not going to dwell on it all that much. Writing travel articles, even good ones, is not as demanding as being a great novelist. I assume if you are holding this book, you are already a decent enough writer to get published or you are in the process of getting there soon on your own. If not, why enter this hyper-competitive, crowded, low-paying field with the deck stacked against you? Go get educated and read this later when you're prepared. Or choose a path of less resistance.

*Travel Writing 2.0* will cover some of the 10 percent of writing well that is unique to travel (and is unique to appealing to search engines, which is not covered in most writing books). Otherwise this is a handbook for the business and marketing side of things, where most of your effort will be concentrated, rather than the construction of subjects, verbs, and adjectives into readable sentences. The resource section lists other good travel writing books that take the opposite approach and I suggest you pick up one of those as well at some point.

As many writers will tell you in these pages, the best way to learn is to constantly practice, stretch, refine, and improve. Thanks to the digital media world, all that is far easier than it used to be. You no longer need to get past a gatekeeper to tell your story.

## The Fun Stuff

Everyone I meet thinks I have a job that's barely one step removed from a wish granted by a genie. "Wow, how did you pull that off?" they'll ask, incredulous, like I just told them I'd hit four 21s in a row in Vegas after doubling down each time. So I get how fortunate I am to be making a living doing something I am passionate about, traveling the world without having to pay for it all.

This vocation sure beats harvesting lettuce, cleaning toilets, or pouring asphalt. It's not fair to talk about all the hardships and ignore the perks, so yes, there are some great perks. *After* you achieve some level of success, you get invited on free trips or have editors paying your expenses. You get paid to go places most people you know will never visit. You get VIP access, get wined and dined, and you may get to travel in a style you would never be able to afford on your own. If you act like a journalist instead of a lazy hack, you will also see more of a place and its culture than you ever would as a casual tourist.

I could spend pages on tales of my luxury safari in Botswana, drinking my way through the wine regions of Eastern Europe, or kicking back in palatial resorts in Mexico. I've also had mind-blowing experiences hanging out with *sadhus* in India and hiking through the Andes Mountains of South America. If we have a beer together sometime, I'll regale you with all the tales of excess and excitement. Right now though, that's like taking a 16 year-old boy to a strip club. All in good time, but first you need to reach a level of maturity—in this case career maturity.

Most fun jobs invite lots of competition and this fun job is as competitive as any of them out there. With success comes a whole range of wonderful byproducts, but you need the success first before you get the goodies. I hope the information I present here will help you get to that point. Yes, it can be a blast eventually, no doubt about it. But you have to want it bad enough to put in the real time and effort required to get to the payoff.

Nearly all of us travel writers are in this because of a love of exploring new places. I backpacked around the world for years before I ever started making real money as a writer. The travel came first, then the writing, which is how it is for most. If there's not a thrill from the travel that drives you, there are certainly far more lucrative pursuits available to you instead.

# Why me?

I have learned how to do a lot of things from "how to" books. I've learned to invest well, buy real estate overseas, grow vegetables, brew beer, write creative non-fiction, start a business, code HTML, market my own book, teach English overseas, and relocate my family to another country. And yes, nearly 20 years ago I read a book on how to be a travel writer. (*The Travel Writer's Guide* by Gordon Burgett, and apparently it did a good enough job to get me on my way.) My two main questions when deciding whether to plunk my money down on one of these how to books are always, "Why should I trust this person?" and "Does the author know what he/she is talking about?"

So here's why you should trust me.

I've been at this for close to two decades, from part-time to full-time, doing almost every kind of job available to writers—travel and otherwise. This includes writing four books, ghostwriting business books and articles, editing two travel webzines, editing one business webzine, working as an RFP writer, publishing articles in dozens of magazines and newspapers, publishing even more on websites, running multiple travel blogs, writing copy for multiple corporations, and writing for the trades. I appear to know enough to be quoted in a slew of major media outlets each year as a travel destinations expert.

I've won a whole lot of nice awards for articles I've written and all my books are still in print. I'm an author who actually makes money from his books and my travel website company is profitable enough to pay all my bills and support my family. (See my portfolio site at www.TimLeffel.com for the full shebang.) So I think at this point it's safe to say I can do more than talk the talk. Objectively, from both an artistic and financial standpoint, I'm a successful travel writer.

If you look up "travel writing" on Google, my name is in the first two results—out of 74 million. I may not be the foremost authority on the subject, but Google thinks I am. The funny thing is, the #2 entry is my article from a few years ago called "The Seven Myths of Being a Travel Writer." I wasn't ever cut out for being a perky cheerleader I guess.

As I was writing this book I got called for an interview about a cheap destination by a fellow travel journalist I've known for a long time and respect immensely. As we went from the subject at hand to chatting about life and the future she said, out of the blue, "You're one of the real success stories. You've showed people that it's possible to really make it on your own." I was taken aback, especially since I had just looked at the measly balance in my checking account that morning. At the same time I was smiling because of who had said it—a travel editor at the most popular general newspaper in my home country: *USA Today*. Here I am thinking she's got a dream job and she's thinking I'm the definition of success. These are strange times.

Just in case my litany of published work is not enough—which it probably isn't since I'm still just one guy with one set of opinions—I have crowdsourced much of the content for this book. I finished reading the Jeff Jarvis book *What Would Google Do?* right before I started writing this. I decided that it was a pertinent question, so I turned to 52 working travel writers I know and respect to answer some burning questions I had. Then I asked them to provide advice and insight. I then did the same with some editors who hire freelancers or book authors. So if you don't trust my opinions, you've got plenty more to pick from in the following pages. Some of these people are pros who have been full-time travel writers for most of their working lives, some have just been at it a couple years, and others are permanent part-time travel writers who have another source of income.

In different ways, they'll show you how to get to where you might want to go, though the paths might be more meandering than they used to be.

## The Murky Future

The rules are changing fast. The way many successful travel writers earn money has completely changed in the past five years. The people really doing the best are the ones ignoring the traditional paths of depending on others for a check and are charting their own course.

So while this book is big on practical advice, it's not so big on most of the specifics you historically find in travel writing books. The main reason is, the real money is going to the most creative thinkers. They are making their own rules.

If you want easy answers, checklists, and the Yellow Brick Road to success, that period has passed. The writers profiled here have found 52 different routes to happiness as a travel writer. Another batch of writers would present even more routes in the new digital age. We're all finding our way into a future that nobody can see clearly right now.

Just as a great language teacher is a facilitator rather than a lecturer, my goal is to show you what to do so you can go develop your talent and skill as a writer and maybe even an entrepreneur. I and the other writers profiled here are going to give you great tips on how to succeed and make money, but despite what any seminar may promise, there are no shortcuts in this vocation. The only thing that's reliably short is the number of digits on your first year or two of paychecks.

So if you want lots of blueprints to copy for breaking into print media, get a library card and start checking out other tomes on the subject of freelance writing. There are plenty of good ones out there. Instead I'm going to tell you to go find great writing yourself and to actually read it, week after week after week. Then I'm going to tell you to write and write and write, preferably doing a good portion of that online. Then I'm going to tell you to work your butt off on marketing so that people actually read what you've typed.

Hacks wait for shortcuts that they never seem to find. Like true explorers, successful travel writers pull out a machete and a compass and start moving. I'm just handing you the map.

*Travel Writing 2.0* will hopefully inspire you and get you jazzed up, but also prepare you for the real life of a freelance travel writer. It will give you a kick in the seat of the pants sometimes too though, and be the wise advisor telling you to get your answers for your specific situation the way most journalists do: by going and finding them. You'll get lots of collective knowledge and advice in this book, then the next steps are all yours.

Let's take a trip!

# How Do Travel Writers Make Money?

Is there any money in this vocation? Well, there can be. Freelance travel writers make money in one of three ways.

1) They write for someone else and get paid by that organization, with a set fee for a specified amount of work.

2) They run their own publication(s) and earn money the same way organizations do: by selling advertising, selling products, earning a commission on others' products featured in their publication, or earning money for services such as consulting or leading tours.

3) They depend on some combination of numbers 1 and 2.

For most freelance writers, this endeavor is like the set-up of a mom and pop business. Count the revenue, subtract the expenses, and there's your profit. Divide what's left by the hours you worked to figure out the earnings from your efforts.

I'm going to skip the come-on images of lounging in beach chairs, piña coladas in hand, enjoying a life of leisure. At the risk of selling fewer books, I'm going straight to the bottom line: actually earning money from doing this.

So let's start out with reality: unless you are a staff travel writer/editor at a magazine or major newspaper—and I would estimate there are fewer than 250 of those full-time jobs left in the whole English speaking world—then you will be a freelancer or you will run your own enterprise.

If you can score one of those staff jobs, then more power to you. The normal path to that is to intern for nothing while in college, work for really cheap for many years as a junior editor or copywriter, then move up to an actual living when someone else leaves or gets fired. Or you are already the food or lifestyle editor at one publication and you end up making a leap to travel at another publication down the street. But in an annoying irony that can be a real bummer, travel editors don't actually travel that much. They have too much to do in the office.

Every other travel writer—which means probably 98 or 99 out of 100—is self-employed.

So first let that idea sink in and decide if it's for you. Are you comfortable forging your own path and being responsible for your own income? Having all the responsibility on your own shoulders? Not being able to make an accurate household budget because you can't forecast your income?

If you're a "punch the clock and pick up a paycheck" type, you may want to stop reading now and pass this book onto someone else who's just the opposite. Travel writing may look glamorous, but it involves a lot of very real work over a very long period.

Edward Hasbrouck would appear to be a successful writer and author. His book, *The Practical Nomad*, is in its fourth edition. He gets regular work as a writer and his blog gets respectable traffic that leads to ad income. Nothing happened quickly, however. He says, "I had a 'day job' with a travel agency for about 15 years before I got to the point where I am making a living almost entirely from travel writing."

His experience is not at all atypical. Many writers who have been at this for a decade or more are just now getting to the point where this is their "real job." Brad Olsen runs CCC Publishing, with a whole range of books under the imprint, but says, "Do it for the love of writing, don't expect much, work hard and hopefully in a decade you'll be able to support yourself! As in don't give up your day job too soon."

You *can* get paid handsomely for this now and then if you land the right assignment. There are plenty of big feature stories assigned by magazines each month that pay 50 cents to $2 a word. So for 2,000 words the writer is getting between $1,000 and $4,000. Those are the elite assignments though, the ones that generally go to writers with plenty of experience. Expecting that to happen quickly is like a news anchor in Greenville, South Carolina looking at what a Los Angeles anchor makes and expecting the same salary.

A more common fee that a freelancer will get for a story of that length is 5 to 25 cents a word, or $100 to $500. Get into the online world and it can be lower still, to the point where you don't want to even think about what you're earning per word because it's a fraction of a cent. Most freelancers who make good money put together a *lot* of assignments on a regular basis and have regular columns or blog appearances on top.

# The Freelancer's World

*It is not childish to live with uncertainty, to devote oneself to a craft rather than a career, to an idea rather than an institution. It's courageous and requires a courage of the order that the institutionally co-opted are ill equipped to perceive. They are so unequipped to perceive it that they can only call it childish, and so excuse their exploitation of you.*
– David Mamet

Playwright and director David Mamet was speaking to actors in that quote, but it applies to any creative field where people are scrambling for the next gig and piecing together streams of income instead of settling for life in a cubicle. Being a writer is not for the faint-hearted or the easily scared. Showing up each day and getting a paycheck is easy. To pursue the independent path takes real courage and fortitude.

Most travel writers are freelance. They wield a lance—or pen, laptop, or netbook—that is for hire. They sell their output to someone for an agreed-upon price or they run their own business and make money from what appears next to their writing. Or more often in the digital age it's a mix of both.

The travel freelancer's life is not for everyone. It involves lots of yin-yang trade-offs. I've lived through every one of the ups and downs and have the gray hairs to prove it.

- You have freedom, but not much certainty.
- You report to nobody, but there's no mentor in the next room either.
- Your hours are your own, but you end up working more of them than most office drones.
- You can go on vacation when you want, but you often end up working while you're away.
- You can work at home, but you buy all your own supplies and equipment.
- You can pick and choose what you work on, but sometimes that means having no work.
- You don't have to follow someone else's workplace rules, but you have to arrange your own health insurance and fund your own retirement account.

I worked for more than a decade in the corporate world, but I left it for good many years ago and can't imagine ever going back to the constraints of a routine job in a structured environment. I love having control over my life, my career, and what I spend my days working on. That doesn't mean it's always easy though. Every freelancer I know talks about the "financial roller coaster" that comes with the territory: one month of everything going right followed by a two months of not being able to make the checkbook balance. Even the people I know who are making six figures complain about this. Over the course of a year their earnings are great, but some months are just plain tough. It takes serious financial discipline and the ability to be what most people would call "a hustler." (In a good way of course…)

I don't think it's fair to talk about "the job" without talking about what that means for "the life." As successful magazine writer and blogger Alison Stein Wellner says, "There are better ways to make a buck than being a writer, period, and second, there are other subjects to write about that are more lucrative than travel."

If you get one point of reality from this book, let it be this: travel writing is not something to go into because of the potential earnings.

When I asked Doug Lansky, author of many successful travel books, what advice he had for aspiring travel writers, he had this to say: "Make sure you have plenty of money to live off of for about a year or two and work your ass off."

I have no way of knowing what would work for your life situation, but here are a few alternate income sources to consider in the early years to make life easier:

- Any full-time day job
- A second (steadier) source of part-time income
- A spouse with good earnings and benefits
- Social security and retirement income
- Savings that will support you for a year or more while you get ramped up
- Unemployment payments/the dole
- Parents who don't mind you living at home and eating their groceries
- Teaching English overseas by day, writing by night
- Being a teacher or professor who has the whole summer off to travel
- Being a seasonal worker with long stretches of time off to travel.
- Working abroad or moving to a country with a much lower cost of living
- Investment or rental property income

It may seem crazy that I am talking about alternate income sources at the very beginning of this book, but for 95% of the travel writers out there, this is reality. Unless you are charmed and remarkable, or already wealthy, you need to be thinking about where the money will come from that pays the bills for a good while.

The rise of new media has not changed that aspect. If anything it's worse because pay scales are flat or declining if you write for established organizations. There are more ways to make money now, including ones totally in your own hands, but all of them take time to build. Travel writing and overnight success do not go hand in hand. Lonely Planet author and freelancer Paige Penland says, "The key to my success? Having other work, such as editing health care studies, that I can do while living in Central America. I couldn't do it with just travel writing."

There's nothing novel about going through these backup scenarios and figuring out how you'll pay the mortgage or the rent. The same is necessary for wannabe actors, sculptors, musicians, songwriters, and other creative types. As we'll talk about later, you can't expect that anyone owes you an income just because you've declared yourself to be a writer. Electricians and plumbers need a license. Architects need five years of schooling plus an apprenticeship. Cops need to graduate from the academy and prove they can shoot straight. All a travel writer needs to do to claim the title is order business cards from VistaPrint. Some don't even do that—they just sign up with Examiner.com and say they're a writer.

This doesn't mean you are thinking of "something to fall back on" because then you are setting yourself up to "fall back." A better outlook is that you are going to have multiple streams of income and that you will keep building to a point where you are making what you need to be comfortable from just your writing-related activities. For a retired person, that may just mean a few hundred dollars a month on top of Social Security. For a stay-at-home mom or dad, maybe enough to cover the grocery bill. For a full-timer, enough to drop all the other stuff that is not fulfilling. Only you know what the magic number is, but once you know it, work toward that and look at any "falling back" as temporary.

Some writers find the balance by mixing in speaking or consulting jobs. These are generally not pursuits you'll be thinking about in your first few years of travel writing, but it is a part worth considering after you have paid your dues and built up a solid portfolio. Some travel book authors have discovered that doing speeches at colleges and conferences pays a whole lot better than the book did. They show up, engage the audience with some fun stories and good PowerPoint slides, sign some autographs, and get a check. What a gig!

It's a great job if you can get it, but that assumes you're reasonably famous, are seen as an expert, and are a good speaker. That doesn't happen overnight. If you're writing a book, however, it's worth keeping this goal in mind as a possibility. Will this translate to the stage? Will people want to hear more about it in person?

Others spend part of their time writing and part of their time leading tours. Joshua Berman was a Peace Corps volunteer in Nicaragua when he and Randall Wood decided to pitch Avalon Publishing on doing a Moon Handbook for Nicaragua. It was the first truly comprehensive guidebook to the region and they became instant experts. Joshua didn't just use that experience to get more writing work though. He also got his training and certifications in line and started leading adventure tours to Central America.

Beth Whitman, who runs WanderlustAndLipstick.com, leads tours to Bhutan and India, gaining most of her business through her books and the website. You'll hear more from both of them later.

# How Much Do Travel Writers Make—Really?

Some people make very little writing about their travels. Some make a very comfortable living. Take the chart below as an unscientific snapshot of the people I interviewed for this book plus me, but I think if you tracked down 52 working travel writers yourself, you'd probably find a pretty similar income breakdown. Here are the collective annual earnings of the writers quoted in this book.

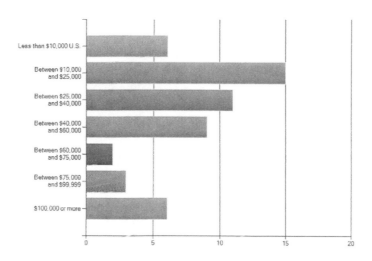

Several data points jump out at me in this chart. The first is that four of the five largest responses are all $60,000 a year or less annually. The second is that there is a big drop-off after that point. The most interesting, however, is that if you get past that dip, the rewards can be great. Ten percent of the writers are making as much as cubicle jockey VPs stressed out in a job they hate, but are reporting to nobody but themselves. That's encouraging.

Keep in mind also that many of the people making less than $25,000 a year are doing that on purpose. They are part-time because they want to be. There's nothing wrong with that and it's a nice place to be if you have another source of income (or a spouse) paying the big bills. Then you can relax and have fun with it.

# What Makes You Special?

To make it as a freelance writer covering any subject, it has always helped to have "a beat," something you can write about better than others. In travel this can mean a subject area, a place, a style of travel, or many other differentiating factors. Being without this—a beat, a niche, a specialty—means you are just another face in the crowd.

My beat, for instance, has traditionally been cheap places to travel and how to travel well on a budget. Later I branched into travel gear that is a good value and I can fairly be considered an expert on both. I am friends with the go-to guys and gals on destinations like Turkey, Mexico, Brazil, Bali, Thailand, Costa Rica, and Guatemala—and I could tell you who to call for 20 other places. If I ever invited all the travel food specialists I know into one place we could have the dinner party of a lifetime. Another acquaintance is an amazing resource on wine and cocktails, another on responsible travel/eco-tourism, and another on traveling with disabilities. These people have a leg up on anyone trying to do it all.

> *I developed an interest in the Outer Banks of North Carolina and put together some articles on the Banks, which I posted online. A travel editor saw the articles, liked them and hired me to do a Frommer's guide to the coast of the Carolinas and Georgia. Although I had freelanced travel articles, this was my first travel book. About the same time, I developed an interest in Belize and began publishing a newsletter and then a magazine on the country. This led to several books, including Fodor's, on Belize. What success I've had I would say comes from my interest in a specific destination, my writing about it and publishing information on that destination, then becoming recognized as an expert on the area, which in turn led to book and article assignments.*
>
> – Lan Sluder, author, writer, and publisher

Writers with a clear focus don't have to try very hard to get assignments or to get quoted as an expert. Anyone who puts the appropriate terms into Google is going to see these people at the top of the rankings. They are therefore recognized as authorities.

So what makes you special? What can you cover better than anyone? For a lot of people that's their own region, but they don't take advantage of it, me included. Here's what Sheila Scarborough, a contributor to Perceptive Travel's blog and the person who runs the Family Travel Guide blog at BootsnAll says: "My best advice? Quit thinking about *going* someplace and pitching stories from there; look around your very own town but see it as a travel writer would, and pitch that. Write what you know. Paris, France has been done. Someone needs to totally rock Paris, Texas."

South Pacific guidebook writer and webmaster David Stanley says if he had it to do all over again, he'd also pay more attention to his own back yard. "I would focus on my local area more and become 'the' expert on it."

Writing about what you know, and where you already live, may go against your idea of "travel writing," but traveling locally has a lot of advantages. You can pitch to regional magazines that aren't inundated with queries. You don't have to get on a plane. You can make local phone calls to reach people and meet them at their office or for coffee. You can change your schedule easily for interviews. You don't need a hotel room. You already know the lay of the land. And this may be the most important factor: people trust you. You are not an outsider who has parachuted in for the weekend; you are a local.

This doesn't mean you have to stay where you are for life and just be a specialist on Fargo, North Dakota. There's still a serious lack of good English language resource sites and blogs once you get beyond the most popular destinations. It wouldn't take long to establish yourself as the travel expert on Mendoza, Zihuatanejo, Moravia, or Sapa. Granted, there's not as much potential in those as being the expert on London, but it's certainly a path of far less resistance. Stake your claim and stick with it.

# Jack of All Trades, Master of One

Eggs in one basket or multiple baskets?

Anyone who depends on a single stream of income from a specific company or even one type of media is going to get a nasty surprise sooner or later. Here's some advice from Beth Whitman, who wears hats as a blogger, publisher, author, and tour leader. "Travel writers must have a multi-pronged approach in order to succeed. It's a small percentage who can actually make a living strictly from their writing. The trick is to be able to channel it all into the travel world so you're not working as a barista during the day (not that there's anything wrong with that) and then blogging and writing at night."

While it's very important to find a niche you can dominate, that doesn't mean a laser focus is going to fatten your bank account, especially in the short term. Even the most specialized writers still have something else they do "on the side," and often that "side" pays their mortgage every month.

I believe strongly that you cannot make it as a freelance writer year after year if you do not have some knowledge or expertise to set you apart. But if there's one thing I can say with certainty about the future of travel writing, it is this: you need to diversify your income streams.

This may sound contradictory, but specialization in a subject area does not mean narrowing your sources of revenue. Be the master of your niche, but find lots of ways to make money from that expertise.

You can pitch articles to local publications and you can pitch to national or international ones as the go-to person for that area or subject. You can blog on that subject or area, attracting readers on your own.

There was a time when one publication you were tight with could keep your bills paid. There was a time when a relationship with a single editor was enough to enable you to sleep well at night. If you're starting off now, however, my advice would be to follow the "multiple streams of income" path instead—the more streams the better. It's just plain reckless to depend on one outlet, one type of media, or one source of advertising income.

Many travel writers also ghostwrite books, do corporate writing, or make a significant portion of their income from advertising running on their own site or blog. Before I went full-time I had a day job as a proposal writer for a tech company, doing my blogging and book writing in the evenings. After that I worked for a while for a national media placement firm where I had complete control over my hours. Both paid better than being a barista, thankfully, since I had a wife and a new daughter to support. The key was, both allowed me the flexibility to pursue my real passion and eventually turn it into my real job.

Holding down a conventional day job while trying to be a travel writer is tough though, especially if you're American and get a pitiful amount of vacation time where you can travel. After all, it's hard to be a travel writer if you only get two weeks off per year unless you can just cover your local region on weekends. Many writers have better luck juggling writing with less structured positions. Teachers have it a little easier:

> *I desired to become a travel writer many years ago when I taught in American International Schools overseas. At that time, I wrote human interest stories for local English newspapers. After teaching, I attended a travel writing workshop in Buenos Aires. My first article came from that experience: "Live Like a Local" was published in EscapeArtist.com. Once I saw my name and photos on the website, I became more confident.*
>
> – Sandra Kennedy, freelance writer

Diversity of income is incredibly important, whether you are making $200 a week from your writing or $2,000. If you take the attitude that any source of income could go away at any time, you will be much better prepared for reality than the person who takes joy in a fat paycheck without considering the future clouds on the horizon. Getting an assignment is great, but that's just the first step: you still need to get paid.

At this point I've done writing work for more startups than I can count. Usually these companies are funded by venture or angel capital and have a sizable budget out of the box. They post an ad or call with a great assignment at a good pay rate and life is good. Eventually, however, reality sets in and those fat paychecks start dwindling. Sometimes the companies go under for good—so watch how much you do up front without getting paid.

Other times I've done work for a reputable magazine, only to see my story die on the vine because the invincible-looking publication is got into financial trouble. As I was writing this book it was happening to a lot of writers who wrote for *Out* magazine and *The Advocate*: many were waiting on checks that were six months overdue. Thankfully the Reader's Digest company doesn't owe me any money for the *Every Day with Rachel Ray* magazine stories I did for the corporation years ago, but that doesn't stop the official-looking bankruptcy proceeding letters from landing in my box each month. That would be demoralizing mail to receive if they still owed me money.

There are two ways to fight this inevitable buzzkill: 1) Run your own show completely or 2) Have multiple streams of income.

I would argue that even #1 requires a bit of #2 because even if you run your own website or blog, your income is from Google, direct ads, networks, affiliate ads, or all of the above. If one of those is half your income, raise the big red flag because what if it goes away?

# Out with the Old: Buggy Whips, Carbon Paper, and Fortress Journalism

*"It breaks my heart to see the trajectory of print media right now. Even though writers can have much greater exposure on the web, the ability to get paid a living wage for your writing has narrowed. Unfortunately, I do not know what the solution to that conundrum is."*
– Laura Laxton, Managing Editor, Northstar Travel Media

At this part of the book, you're probably itching for practical how-to advice. "Where do I start? What do I do right now? Just show me how to turn this career on!"

The thing is, getting to mechanics before we get a look at the landscape will be the equivalent of sending you off to the Amazon jungle without a map or local guide. So before we get to query letters, starting a blog, or how to write a good first paragraph, let's look at how we got here.

In the past, the advice was fairly consistent and tried-and-true. You study the publications that are a good match for ideas you have. Then you send a targeted query to the right editor and wait to hear back. If you get an assignment in all the rejections, you then turn in a well-written piece on time and try to parlay that into more assignments. You start small and build your collection of clippings, thereby getting better and larger assignments as time goes on. Maybe you even get signed up as a guidebook writer, spending months gathering info about a particular destination and turning it into chapters or the whole book.

For more than 50 years, this is how things worked. There were variations on this theme, with trade magazines, staff editorial positions, and narrative books offering other paths, but in the end they all depended on you getting a yes from a powerful gatekeeper—an editor, agent, or publisher.

Some have called this fortress journalism, which is an apt description. Everything we readers were fed in the pre-internet age was controlled by gatekeepers and publishers in their mighty towers. You either played by their rules or you didn't play at all. It didn't matter how much talent you had or what kind of great ideas you had if you didn't get to the right people and get them to listen. If you sucked at writing short and cutesy "front of the book" articles but were brilliant at writing feature stories, well too bad. You weren't allowed to skip to C without going through A and B. If you had so much info to share that people would line up to hear your advice, it didn't matter if the gatekeepers didn't want to give you a forum.

Those days are not completely gone and if you want to break into the elite magazines or the *New York Times*, it still might as well be 1950 rather than 2010. With print media, the only things that have changed are that you use e-mail instead of the postal service and in inflation-adjusted dollars they are paying you far less than they used to pay. Oh, and you don't have to make duplicate Ektachrome slides and mail them with fingers crossed. Otherwise it's all about working your way up a ladder slowly, building relationships (while praying the editor who hired you doesn't get fired), building up a portfolio, and trying to snag better assignments over time.

Financially, it can be a tough slog. As you can imagine, this is no way to make a living from the get-go. I'd say 8 out of every 10 travel writers I know spent at least a year getting established before they made more than a good night's bar tab from an article. Most spent many years, working another job at the same time, doing this on the side, or using severance/savings/a spouse to support them while they built up a body of work. Most of the exceptions are people who got a staff job: the intern who became a junior editor with a salary; the junior copy editor who worked her way into the travel section; the guidebook company minion who moved out from behind a desk to go research a guidebook on a place nobody else wanted to go.

There's hope though. In the past few years, a new route has opened up, one that is self-directed and has nothing to do with getting buy-in from an editor or publisher. It's an entrepreneurial path, a marketing path, and a path requiring greater discipline, but it's one that depends on pleasing an audience of readers, not pleasing one busy person in a cramped Manhattan office. Some people in this book are still 100% on the old path, some are 100% on one of the branches of the new path. The majority are somewhere in between, trying to figure out how to optimize the mix. You'll meet a lot of them in this book and hear their stories.

Before we look at the future though, where are we right now? What's wrong with all those books on travel writing 1.0? The media in place since World War II is fading fast. We are in the midst of a major transformation, one not seen since the mass adoption of television. That was 50 years ago.

Print will probably never really go away; video didn't really kill the radio star after all—at least for the radio star who could adapt. But writing for newspapers and magazines is looking less dependable every month. Here's a look at how serious things got just in the last year of the oughts (00s) in the second millennium:

- The Reader's Digest corporation filed for bankruptcy and Europe's largest media company—Bertelsmann—reported its first annual net loss in 30 years.

- In early 2010, Yahoo's market value was more than all the following added together: New York Times company, Washington Post company, Gannett Publishing (USA Today and 85 other newspapers), E.W. Scripps TV channel company, McClatchy, Media General, and CBS. (And Yahoo is worth a fraction of Google.)

- A slew of magazines went under including *National Geographic Adventure, Gourmet, Vibe, Far Eastern Economic Review, Town & Country Travel, Hallmark Magazine, Travel & Leisure Family, Travel & Leisure Golf, Best Life, Modern Bride, Plenty, Jewish Living, Nickelodeon*

*Magazine, Domino, Country Home, Teen,* and…*Goats Across Canada.*

- Several other magazines went digital-only, including *AdWeek,* the *Hollywood Reporter,* and just about every magazine having something to do with tech (except glorious *Wired,* thankfully).

- More than 100 newspapers folded and a few major ones in markets such as New York, Chicago, Detroit, San Francisco, and Boston teetered on the brink of financial collapse. The newspaper industry shed 86,800 jobs in just 12 months.

- Britain's *The Independent* newspaper sold for £1 plus assumption of debts.

- The Washington Post company put *Newsweek* magazine up for sale after saying it "saw no way to turn a profit" with the publication.

- The Condé Nast offices were going through so many budget cuts that there were rumors staffers had to bring their own coffee stirrers to the office. They cut pay for some articles at Condé Nast Traveler by 20% after ad pages dropped by an unprecedented 41%.

- Adult hardcover book sales were down 18% and paperback sales were down 14% in 2009.

- The Borders group closed 200 of its 330 Waldenbooks mall stores at the start of 2010. In some towns that meant the closing of the only bookstore since two of every three independent bookstores open in 1990 are now gone.

Some of this can be chalked up to a bad economy and ad sales will pick up somewhat when the recession ends. But will print media ever recover from the blow? It feels like we're collectively moving on, already seeing print publications as yesterday's news.

Statistics Canada's Survey of Household Spending found that average spending on periodicals was around $60 per household, from 1999 to 2005. From 2006 to 2008 (the latest numbers available), spending on periodicals declined to $47 per household. The US Department of Labor says that American households spent $97 in 1999 on newspapers and magazines and only $61 in 2008. In both cases it's probably even lower now. Think about it: that annual expenditure is less than the average voice and data plan *monthly* bill for someone with an iPhone or Blackberry. So how important is print media in the average person's life?

There is a sea change happening that does not bode well for the future of newspapers and magazines. Readers are moving to the web and advertisers are following them. Without readers or advertisers, what does a publication have left? Editors apparently agree. In a survey conducted by Pew Research in 2010, 48 percent of the editors who participated said that "without a significant new income stream, their organizations could not remain solvent for more than 10 years; 31 percent gave them five years or less."

They can move the whole operation online, as some have done already, but without the scarcity that fortress journalism created, they can't earn nearly as much money there. Instead of competing with their peers, they are competing with everyone—and usually "everyone" includes a few good one-person websites with similar traffic levels but 1/100th of the overhead.

In the print world, England has a handful of newspapers that still publish robust travel sections and a there are a few travel magazines that matter. Go online though and there are probably hundreds of travel blogs and websites just based in England—with free content. Cross the ocean to the United States and the difference expands exponentially: maybe 40 travel magazines that still have a sizable readership (counting regional ones and airline magazines), but probably at least 2,000 travel content websites and blogs with decent enough traffic to get significant advertising—and growing every month.

When faced with those numbers, how can *Travel & Leisure* charge advertisers a premium for their web traffic like they do for their magazine spreads? Sure, they're a recognized brand, but some travel websites that weren't even around five years ago get more traffic and their readers stick around longer. It's a different media world now and the big publishing brands just don't have the power or influence they once did.

Travel media is still incredibly important. By some estimates travel itself is the biggest industry in the world by revenue. People are reading more about travel than they ever did in the past. Exotic places that nobody used to visit are now hot destinations. That's all very positive. But now there are most places to get information and that information is sliced and diced into smaller subsets that better fit varying needs. The pie has expanded, but it has thousands more pieces.

We can fight this trend or we can embrace it. Embracing it means recognizing all the sliced-up micromarkets and anticipating where the new ones are headed. It means capitalizing on the new hunger for more specific information. Fifteen years ago, how many publications talked about eco-tourism, voluntourism, gay tourism, or medical tourism? Who was taking a vacation in Croatia, Nicaragua, or Cambodia? Five years ago, who needed information on the best travel apps for the iPhone or which airlines were reaming customers the most on baggage fees and fuel surcharges?

Nobody. There wasn't a big enough market to support these niches when all info was in print, or the niches didn't even exist. On the web, writers can meet those specific information needs and make money from being a trusted resource. The people answering the new questions are getting lots of readers as a result.

## What About Books?

In the book publishing world the readership decline is less dramatic, but it's still ugly. No matter what developed country you look at, book readership is down, and from a base that was already pretty low to start with. Couple that with a ridiculously inefficient distribution system and you've got a situation where as few as 20% of all books released turn a profit—including travel guidebooks. All the ones that don't sell get recycled at best or go into a landfill at worst, after being shipped back and forth to several warehouses and stores before that point, burning more fossil fuel. The vast majority of authors are lucky if they end up making more for their time spent on a book than a teenager stocking shelves in a supermarket.

Fortunately, there may be more hope here than with other traditional media. If electronic books can become accepted the way digital music has been accepted—without the piracy part—then there's some chance for a plateau at least rather than a sharp decline. Plus the new book landscape is much more tilted in the author's favor than the old one.

> *My publisher of many years is having to cut back on "my" regularly updated books (e.g.* Work Your Way Around the World) *due to falling sales, so the amount of work and therefore income from that source is decreasing.*
>
> – Susan Griffith, journalist and author

Nothing is assured however and only one of the publishers I contacted for this book gets more than five percent of its revenue from electronic media. More than half agreed with the statement, "Overall travel book sales will continue to decline each year."

Another worrisome answer that popped up far more than I expected was, "We don't pay advances." What? I'm supposed to write a whole book without any commitment that you'll pay me for it upon release? What kind of business are you running Mr. Publisher?

This means you are signing away your rights to a book, getting only 10-15% of the income, yet taking the bulk of the risk yourself. Sure, the publisher has costs related to formatting and printing, but you're the one who slaved away months of your time to create the product. From a business standpoint, this makes no sense, especially since the author does the bulk of the promotion as well.

More and more, smaller publishers are blurring the lines between traditional and print-on-demand, passing all of the risk onto the authors, with no payment up front. Will they go the way of music labels as a result, relegated only to the superstar acts and those needing full-blown retail distribution? We'll see, but just as many rock bands now fill 2,000-seat venues without being attached to a major label, authors are finding they can do better on their own than by signing a lopsided contract with a book publisher and getting very little in return.

If you have a good platform, the future could turn out to be a brighter time to be a non-fiction book author than any time in the past. It's a terrible time to be a music label executive, but a great time to be a band with a following. It's probably soon going to be a terrible time to be a book publishing executive, but a great time to be an author—*if* you're good at marketing. As we'll explore in more depth later, being good at marketing is more important now than it has ever been for writers.

## The Changing Definition of "Writing"

Futurist and professor Marshall McLuhan coined the saying, "The medium is the message" and the internet age has magnified his point. People consume information very differently on a computer monitor than they do in a magazine or newspaper. They consume it differently still on a small portable smartphone. When communicating on Twitter and Facebook, they have the attention span of a fruit fly. From a writer's standpoint, it is hard to see any of this as a positive development. When reading electronic articles, attention spans are shorter, people do more skimming, and they are searching for answers more than reading for enjoyment or enrichment.

Some publications defy this trend—and profit by being different—but in general writing for the web requires adjustments. The engaging lede (often referred to as "the lead") meant to draw readers in often gives way to a paragraph stuffed with keywords for the search engines. An article that would go on interrupted for two pages now requires subheads to break it up. There's no easy way to insert the kind of information-packed sidebar you see in newspapers and magazines. There's a limit to how large and how detailed photos can be.

Conversely, the web has lots of advantages. It's searchable. There are hyperlinks. You can insert video. You can match ads to the content. There's an infinite supply of pages to hold the content. Stories live on forever instead of being tossed in the recycling bin when the next issue arrives.

So what does it mean to be a good writer in this environment? It depends on the medium. In a later chapter we'll break it down by outlet type.

## Survive or Thrive

Maybe for another three to five years the old guard of print writers can keep doing what they've always been doing. There will still be some writers who get enough big feature assignments from surviving magazines (especially trade magazines) to still do well. The really great ones can probably keep going strong for a decade or more if they get a steady stream of book royalties and speaking gigs.

This is the path of most resistance for a new writer, however, like studying to be a buggy whip maker just as Henry Ford was revving up his factories.

> *I happened to be sitting at a conference table with three or four twenty-somethings recently and at one point we went around the table to list some of the markets we contributed to. After my turn came and I reeled off my outlets, there was a confused silence. "Oh," said one girl finally. "Print!?!" I guess that, as a guy who writes for newspaper sections and a few magazines, I'm a Stegosaurus. But instead of trying to evolve like smarter writers and do stuff for websites or start my own blog, I'm still lumbering along eating the same ferns in the same forest. My guess is that three years from now I'll be well on my way to becoming extinct."*
>
> – Peter Mandel, travel journalist and author

For those who want to excel in the new digital world, a whole different mindset is required. The old way of building up clips, establishing a track record, and getting cozy with a few key editors is going to be less and less effective. Some will still manage it as a print-only freelancer, others will get staff positions, but most will need to either give up or find another way.

The old model will eventually go the way of Windows 2000. Like it or not, it's time for Travel Writing 2.0.

# In with the New: Unleashing the Writing Entrepreneurs, the Solopreneurs, and the Gig Creators

*If you want to write the fortunes for the cookies that don't exist anymore, you may need to make your own organization, lead your own tribe and hire yourself.*
– Seth Godin

So if old media outlets—and their nice paychecks—are fading fast, what is replacing them? As far as money goes, that's still an open question. Most websites don't pay anything close to what comparable print publications pay, primarily because what they are earning in revenue isn't close to what a healthy print magazine pulls in on a monthly basis. Plenty of people I know are making great money as a new type of travel writer, but most of them are content owners, not just writers.

Like it or not, the era of "user-generated content" has also devalued the worth of the written word. We're all drowning in words and can only consume a fraction of even what interests us the most. TripAdvisor has more pages posted than most other travel sites added together—and they haven't paid for any of the content. By the time you read this, Yelp will have probably passed the 10 million reviews milestone, all of them posted by volunteers who wanted to rant or rave—typos and bad grammar be damned.

Getting mad at all these people who "write for free" and devalue the work of those who want to get paid for it is a fruitless exercise. The genie is certainly already out of the bottle and it likes the fresh air.

To survive in the new media landscape, you'd be wise to go back and study Charles Darwin. "It is not the strongest of the species that survives, nor the most intelligent that survives. It is the one that is the most adaptable to change."

Those who are really "making it" as a travel writer and feel confident about their futures are those who are adapting best to the new reality. They are finding ways to meld their skills to new demands and markets.

That's not easy, no matter what anyone's *Make a Fortune Blogging in Your Underwear* e-book may tell you. If you're going down this road, expect plenty of detours, breakdowns, and potholes along the way. In other words, a good road trip—if you have the right attitude.

Of the writers I surveyed for this book, nearly two-thirds are still making the majority of their income from work they do for others. I'm guessing that percentage will decline each year this book is out going forward. No matter where the money comes from though, the equation is the same: make enough revenue to be left with a profit.

## Economics and Accounting for Freelance Writers

Making money as a writer entails understanding the same basic formula that guides all types of freelance or self-employed work:

$$r-e=p$$

That's revenue minus expenses equals profit. In the real world that formula can get much more complicated in a hurry, for example:

$$(r1+r2+r3)-(e+o+t)=p$$

That would be revenue from three stories minus travel expenses, office costs, and taxes. What's left is what you actually earned. Take it further as a full-time freelancer though and you also have to factor in real living expenses, pesky costs like housing, health insurance, and food.

"Hey egghead, I'm a writer not a math whiz," you're probably thinking. Well too bad. You had better get good at understanding your finances to be a freelancer or you won't have anything that equals "p" in that equation. (Of course if you are completely supported by a spouse or retirement income—more on that later—then you can stay blissfully unconcerned about how much you actually earn.)

In simple terms, the goal is to make more money than you spend. If you finance your own trips and write for tiny publications—or are a blogger—it's tough to make that formula look positive. It's noble, but in a starving artist kind of way. If you're paying for your own travels and writing, it's usually more sane to look at those earnings as gravy, a byproduct, not as your main source of income. Otherwise you'll find you are permanently in the red.

Here are a few things travel writers do to make the formula work out so that p=real **profits**.

1) Write for publications that pay expenses. In these situations you agree on what it will cost, you submit expenses to an editor, and you get reimbursed.
2) Go on press trips or accept hosting from tourism bureaus and hotels.
3) Cover the local region so expenses are far lower.
4) Make sure the article or guidebook project fee is higher than what will be spent.
5) Write for a self-owned publication where ad income is higher than expenses

We collectively have to get better at understanding basic economics. If TravelKingpin.com makes $2 a page per month on the article you wrote for them from advertising, they're not about to pay you big bucks for your article, even if it's great and even if you turn in another 99 great ones. They'll probably pay you a fraction of what they are bringing in—which in this case is only $200 a month from your 100 articles. If you run your own site though and average $2 a month from each of 100 pages, your revenue actually *is* $200. That's still not much, but it's yours and it'll keep being yours every month, increasing as your traffic goes up. TravelKingpin.com is not evil. It's a business. In general terms, the site is not going to pay you more money than the revenue you generate. Their risk, their reward. If you work for yourself, you take all the risk and reap a higher reward.

If you understand this basic tradeoff, you can evaluate opportunities in a better light. JoeNobodyBlog.com may only pay you a few dollars a post. One that's more established may do a revenue share or pay you $6-$10 a post. An established blog network funded by venture capitalists may pay you $15 for 200-400 words. Keep moving up the ladder and you get $50-$100 for a real article or corporate blog post. Get into the rarified air where major sites pull in millions of visitors and you start getting closer to the print world, like $200 to $1,000 for a quality piece that will get read by hundreds of thousands of visitors.

That range goes from peanuts to the monthly rent, but all of these options can make sense for the right person at the right time and I'll admit that I've done work for all of the above. Sure, I'd rather have $1,000 than $6, but compensation takes many forms and the dollar amount is just one of them. In my case I took the low-paying blog posting jobs because I wanted an outlet for something specific, I wanted a valuable link back to my sites (more on that later), I knew it would sell books, or it helped me help someone who helped me. (More on that last one later too.) Any gig can be a good gig if it serves a purpose for you, especially when you are just starting out as a writer.

I am also firmly in the camp that believes what Malcolm Gladwell proposed in *Outliers*: most people who are great at something have spent at least 10,000 hours practicing. Think about that number. It equates to about three years and five months of writing eight hours a day, seven days a week. Or about five years if you work at it 40 hours a week and don't take many vacations. (And don't spend half your day sending glorified text messages on Facebook and Twitter.)

Still, compared to some activities, 10,000 hours is not all that daunting. Clay Shirkey, author of *Cognitive Surplus*, estimates that a person born in 1960 has spent five times that amount sitting passively in front of a television. That's more than five and a half solid *years* of a 50-year-old's life. The obvious lesson: turning off the TV is a great first step in becoming a better writer.

Ask any writer who has been at it for a decade or two and most will tell you, "I'm still improving." For me, the best story I ever wrote came out last year. But I'll probably write something better this year. Then I'll improve again the year after that.

Write often, write a lot, write about different things in different styles—that's how you become great. So those who evaluate every potential job by whether it's going to cover the car payment or not are going to lose out on a lot of valuable practice, practice that comes with immediate (and sometimes brutal) feedback.

*After I graduated from college in Virginia, I moved to Riga, Latvia and took a job at an English-language newspaper called The Baltic Observer. There, I discovered that I preferred writing funny tourist guides to covering austere matters of government and finance. From Riga, I moved to New York and held various jobs as a financial journalist, but I always wanted to get back into travel writing. That opportunity came when I noticed that Gawker media had launched a travel blog called Gridskipper. I got in touch with the editor and began contributing stories. After Gridskipper relaunched under a different format, I moved over to Jaunted, a similar pop culture travel blog. I'm now the weekend editor of Jaunted, which is an enjoyable part-time gig where I have the freedom to write whatever I like, as long as it's interesting.*

*I also contribute stories to two other travel websites. All of this is on top of a full time job at Black Book, as well as having a three-year-old son, so you can be sure I'm always sleep deprived. The keys to my success were reaching out to editors, making clear that I wanted to write for them, and following up. Having my own personal blog helped in developing web publishing/photo/video/HTML skills. Beyond that, I've tried to approach subjects from unique angles, ask questions that haven't been asked yet, and speak in my own voice rather than relying on sun-dappled clichés. And yeah, you've got to work your ass off. Forget TV at night, you write.*

– Victor Ozols

Victor Ozols' meandering path is actually more typical than any straight one in today's media world. In an environment where it's increasingly hard to make a living from just one or two outlets—or even one or two kinds of media—hustling for multiple income sources is key.

Part of being a financially savvy freelancer is also making sure the organization you are writing for can actually pay you. Before, freelance writers didn't think much about the financial health of the publications they were writing for; you got the assignment and were happy to have the work. Most of us have gotten burned at least once by a magazine that crashed and burned, taking the I.O.U.s with it to the graveyard. In the new climate we have to be more vigilant about dying print publications—even century-old newspapers that once seemed invincible—and also web start-ups that could disappear as fast as they began.

I started this chapter with a quote from Seth Godin and I'm going to end with another one. If you're running your own show as a solopreneur or business owner, you probably ought to have his blog at the top of your RSS reader and be looking at every post. He gets his ideas across a few paragraphs at a time, without a lot of wasted words. That's a good model for any writer.

*Just because you're good at something doesn't mean the market cares any longer.*

*The Marx Brothers were great at vaudeville. Live comedy in a theatre. And then the market for vaudeville was killed by the movies. Groucho didn't complain about this or argue that people should respect the hard work he and his brothers had put in. No, they went into the movies.*

*Then the market for movies like the Marx Brothers were making dried up. Groucho didn't start trying to fix the market. Instead, he saw a new medium [television] and went there.*

- SethGodin.typepad.com

# The 52 Faces of a Travel Writer

*It's still a mystery to me how most travel journalists make money.*
- Randy Curwen, Travel Editor, Chicago Tribune

What does it mean to be a "travel writer" in the second decade of the new millennium? Articles writer or editor? Book author or webmaster? Blogger or corporate writer? There's no one answer that is going to work for everyone.

**Jeff Greenwald** was one of my heroes when I first started reading narrative travel books and I've been fortunate enough to feature a few of his stories at Perceptive Travel. He got his start living in New York after his first long-term visit to Asia in the mid-1980's, making contacts at higher-profile magazines and eventually publishing stories in magazines like *Via* and *Islands*. He later went on to write a string of books, including the well-known *Shopping for Buddhas*, but as I'll discuss later, being a book author results in more glory than money. You can still catch his stories in *Islands* and *Afar*. Regarding the future he says, "I have virtually no idea how much travel writing will be a part of my career in one year, let alone three. With any luck I'll publish another book and can be less reliant on the magazine racket!"

**Amy Rosen** had a magical start in travel writing. "I was always an avid traveler, but as a freelance journalist I never thought to actually write stories and earn money from my travels. I just thought those two compartments were separate. (Not sure why.) About 10 years ago I got back from a trip to the Galapagos with a few friends, and one of my journalist friends said: 'You should write about it.' And so I did. The next week, that story took up two full pages of the travel section in the Winnipeg Free Press, plus a full page photo I took on the cover of the section. And away I went. Since then, my travel writing, with a focus on food—my forte—has been like a tree, with regular gigs branching out from the trunk of the first few outlets that would have me."

Amy has won a whole slew of writing awards and is a regular at many Canadian newspapers and magazines. "Over the past few years I've been focusing more on magazine features, but I've been lucky to do so as I realize most of those gigs are drying up; I just happen to be regular with a few still-thriving publications."

**Nicholas Gill** also came to travel writing by way of food. "I was a budding food writer that, after graduating from college, began to travel quite a bit so the transition was somewhat natural. The key to my success has been to just keep trying. I've had far more rejection letters than acceptance letters in queries and pitches, but you learn from that." He travels across Latin America on a regular basis and his work appears in publications such as *The New York Times, National Geographic Traveler, Condé Nast Traveler, Caribbean Travel & Life*, and *LuxuryLatinAmerica*.com

He has also authored numerous guidebooks on Latin American countries for Frommer's and other publishers. In 2009, he launched an e-zine on Latin American food, drink, and travel, New World Review (www.newworldreview.com)

**Beth Whitman** broke into travel writing with a multi-pronged approach. "I wrote a book, *Wanderlust & Lipstick*, to establish myself as an authority in the world of women's travel and then launched a website and blog to help promote the books." Beth has parleyed that expert status into a line of other books she publishes herself and a business running tours to India and Bhutan. She has turned WanderlustandLipstick.com into a full platform, hiring other bloggers to write different sections of the site. Writing has become just a piece of the whole, as much a marketing tool as an income source. "As other parts of my business grow (namely tours), I think that my writing will continue to be less of a revenue generator and more of a means to help promote and sell the Wanderlust and Lipstick tours."

**Alison Stein Wellner** says she sidled into travel writing. "I had many years under my belt of writing about other subjects—I've been a full-time freelancer for 13 years, but have only been focusing exclusively on travel for the past three years. I was writing a lot for business magazines, so when I decided I wanted to focus on travel, I started to pitch travel ideas to business magazines. I focused first on business travel, then on luxury travel, and I kept going from there." Her print credits run from *Inc.* to *New York Magazine* to airline magazines and she blogs for multiple outlets.

**Gary Arndt** started his now-successful Everything-Everywhere.com blog when he began traveling around the world half a decade ago. It's something many people do when they take off, but Gary kept at it and turned his blog into a full-time job, now making enough to pay his bills and support his globetrotting. "The keys to my success have been internet marketing and constant attention to the site," he says. "I don't view myself as a travel writer. I view myself as a travel blogger. At no point have I ever considered writing for someone else for money."

**John DiScala** (a.k.a. Johnny Jet) was one of the travel website pioneers but says he just got lucky. "I used to be afraid to fly. I started learning all kinds of tips and began helping others' travels." He put up one of the original travel resource websites and it took off. He now flies around 150,000 miles and visits over 20 countries each year. He and his website JohnnyJet.com have been featured over 1,800 times in major publications, including most of the major U.S. media outlets.

He has what many would consider a dream job: he travels around wherever he wants to go and writes about his trips. He makes serious money as a travel writer, but not because of the articles he writes for others—that part is gravy. He makes his living from advertisers who want to be a part of his site. He got on the Web early and has staked out a strong position with lots of readers, but kept the momentum going by continuing to keep those readers and add new ones.

The strategy employed by Gary and Johnny—the last two on that list—is the common thread among most of the financially successful travel writers I know: they write for themselves and own their content instead of giving it away to others for one-shot article fees. But as the examples above illustrate, "travel writers" have many different faces. You'll hear stories and advice from some of the other 52 throughout this book.

For some, it's not really about the money, and that's fine. As I was starting this book I got invited on a blogger summit sponsored by Gore-tex. They flew a bunch of us to their headquarters, wined and dined us a couple nights, and taught us about their product lines. Yes, I got some cool gear to try out—which of course I reviewed later. (For more on the ups and downs of press junkets, see the Perks and Profits chapter).

Outdoor apparel companies have been way ahead of travel destinations in understanding the power of the web and this summit was a great example. Only three of the 16 people invited were full-time writers. One was a geologist, one worked for a TV network, one had a communications job with a big software company, and one worked at a gear retail shop.

The thing is, they all ran influential blogs or websites that had gotten onto Gore's radar. These people ran some of the most respected sites around on mountain biking, snowboarding, skiing, hunting, rock climbing, and backcountry hiking. (And in my case, a blog about useful travel gear.) Some of these writers were making serious money from their sites, while others were barely making enough to buy a season pass to a ski resort. The common denominator was that they were all passionate about their particular niche and had become known influencers—industry experts. For many people, that's enough.

I met Jennifer Miner and Kara Williams at a conference called Travel Media Showcase a few years ago and have kept in touch with them ever since, even hiring Kara to be one of my reviewers at Practical Travel Gear. They are two of the founders/writers at TheVacationGals.com, a family travel blog. Neither of them is getting rich from their efforts and they both contribute to a long list of different publications, but the writing from that site and others provides both a good income stream while letting them get some nice perks and write about what they enjoy. Jennifer says, "The web has been, and continues to be, a great source for novice travel writers. There are many sites that accept "newbies," where we can learn the ropes as freelancers—despite the low wages therein."

Kara broke into travel writing by "covering her own backyard," writing $25 articles for GoColorado.com. She also wrote for free for BellaOnline.com covering honeymoon travel. "I took my travel writing career up a notch by taking an online course from Amanda Castleman. Soon after I landed more lucrative web and print assignments."

> *In the past 6 months, I ceased contributing to any newspaper outlets, primarily because some closed down and others were asking for major pay cuts. Right now, I'm about 50/50 print vs. online. I'm still finding plenty of print clients that will pay me $1/word, but have diversified with several daily blogs. The pay is slightly lower than I'd like, but I can bang out a 250-word blog post with my eyes closed in a relatively short amount of time. There's something refreshing about instant online editorial gratification and I don't mind writing the shorter pieces. If that's the new future of online edit, I should have no problem adapting.*
>
> - Charyn Pfeuffer, freelance writer

## Does Location Matter?

For a freelance writer, location used to matter a lot. There's a good reason half the working magazine writers seem to live in New

York City: it's the biggest publishing center in the world. Apart from a few outlier magazines like *Outside, Wend,* and *Southern Living,* most editors work in Manhattan. So do most book publishers and literary agents. So do a whole slew of organisms that depend on these industries, like PR agencies, ad agencies, and tourism boards. The same goes for London if you're a British writer or Sydney if you're Australian.

Whenever I return to New York, I understand the allure of living there. It's a blur of parties, of event invitations, of rubbing elbows with people that matter. Last time I visited the city for a conference, author David Farley talked me into going to a party a liquor PR company was sponsoring. In a city I hadn't been to for two years, a place I hadn't lived in for more than a decade, I ran into four people I knew within a half hour of arriving. The Six Degrees of Separation principle is in overdrive in Manhattan.

The problem is, it's really ridiculously expensive to live in New York City. Your normal American spends less on a mortgage for a three-bedroom house with a yard than most New Yorkers spend on rent for a cramped studio apartment. You get invited to parties, but good thing because you don't have money to buy booze on your own. You have a better chance of meeting editors, but you need lots and lots of assignments from them just to cover your expenses.

As print media becomes less and less important, it follows that living in New York (or London)

> *In person meetups have helped a lot, whether it is meeting with local travel bloggers here in Seattle, or attending conferences where I meet established travel writers and travel bloggers from around the country. It's important to spend time developing relationships with other bloggers and writers who are just starting out and with writers who are more established.*
>
> – Debbie Dubrow, family travel blogger

will matter less and less. As digital media has become more and more influential, we're seeing writers live where they can afford to live instead of living where they feel like they have to live. When nearly every communication is by e-mail, why do you need to even be in a city? Rolf Potts seems to do fine on a farm in Kansas. For that matter, why do you even need to be in your home country? I have freelancers working for me who are living in Costa Rica, Mexico, New Zealand, Australia, and Chile.

I'm one of those people who thinks the fragmentation of media is a healthy development. As someone who lived and worked in the New York City area for many years, I know first-hand how myopic a place it is. There's a tremendous amount of group-think going on and most New Yorkers will freely admit they have no grasp of how people in the rest of the country live or what motivates them. So it will probably help us all if the media decision making gets spread out to a wider base. I'm thrilled to see all the new travel magazines setting up shop elsewhere, like *Wend* in Portland and *Afar* in San Francisco.

The beautiful thing about the environment we are transitioning toward now is that location doesn't matter much. Why do you need a New York or London publisher if most of your books will sell through Amazon and Apple? Why does your website need to be in a major city if you are posting from the road or a home office anyway, not even knowing where your server is located? Why do you need to be rubbing shoulders with editors in their home town if most of your income is derived from content you own yourself?

By the time this book comes out, I'll be putting my money where my mouth is, doing everything I do now from Guanajuato, Mexico. A year later I'll move back to the states, but it doesn't really matter where. In the age of blogs, e-mail, Skype, IM, apps, YouSendIt, WordPress, and Twitter, who cares where you plug in your laptop? You can adjust your expenses to enable the pursuit of your dream.

The one caveat to this is, the solitary life of a writer becomes more solitary—in a physical sense anyway—if there's no community of writers around you. I've never met another travel writer living in my home town of the past decade, Nashville. If you live in Seattle or

San Francisco, however, you can't toss a hacky sack in a coffee shop without hitting one.

If having a community of people to meet with and bounce ideas off of is important, move to a place where your type already lives. With a little effort you'll have a built-in support group.

Otherwise, live wherever you want and get on a plane to attend conferences and go on group press trips. Then stay in touch with the people you have met in person: often those bonds are much stronger and longer-lasting than those established with an online avatar.

## The Key Qualities of a Travel Writer

You cannot spot a travel writer in an airport like you can a pilot, a pro basketball player, or a priest. There's no uniform, no typical physique, and no telltale sign of a specific profession. Except for times when you'll see one taking notes in a notebook, there are few clues projected through appearance or action.

There are some common characteristics the good ones have in common though, qualities that separate the winners from the losers across all kinds of travel writers. If you don't have a good number of the following in your personal arsenal, start working on them now. Otherwise you are going to struggle.

**Self-motivated.** I think it's safe to say that all writers covering any subject have their moments of self-doubt and it's hard to not feel you have some faults when editors repeatedly reject your ideas. We get over it though because we have to. Like a great salesperson who measures success by the number of times he hears "no" in a day, a freelance writer needs to have the motivation to keep plugging away to score the next assignment or pull in that next batch of subscribers. It's very easy to get discouraged, which is why the self-motivated writers are the ones still working ten years after they started, while others give up and move on to another vocation that's less of a struggle.

**Persevering.** Motivation can't be fleeting and temporary. The writer who perseveres and keeps at it is the one who will succeed after the others have dropped out. This is true in traditional media, where you are pitching to editors, and in the blogging world, where most writers make little to no money in their first six months or a year of work. "Instant success" is so rare as to be statistically impossible in the travel writing world. It takes a long view and perseverance to survive and eventually thrive.

**Flexible and Adaptable.** If you've ever been a backpacker for months or a year on end, you've got this one down already. Travel is, by nature, unpredictable. Things go wrong on a regular basis. There are a lot of moving parts on any journey: airlines, ground transportation, a parade of hotels, attractions, restaurants, people to interview, and places where you can log on to the internet—for a start. You roll with the punches when things fall through and learn to adapt. Quoting Darwin again, "In the long history of humankind (and animal kind, too) those who learned to collaborate and improvise most effectively have prevailed."

This need for flexibility also applies to the actual writing. Different publications require a different style and voice. An editor may make changes to your article that you don't agree with, but she is the boss so you learn to live with it. That angle you had so carefully researched before leaving may turn out to be a crappy angle once you've arrived and you need to change course. Roll with it.

**Confident.** If you don't believe in yourself and your abilities, there are hundreds of people out there ready to supply negative feedback. There are also hundreds of more confident writers ready to leapfrog over you at any given time. This doesn't mean your story is great when every editor has told you it's awful, but if you've got a reason to believe you're a good writer—from classes, writing groups, awards, publication credits, blog traffic—then exude that confidence and use it to energize your efforts. There is no shortage of people who will write nasty blog comments, ignore your e-mail pitches, tell you you're crazy to try to make it as a writer, or ask when you're going to get a real job. If you don't have the confidence to deflect all that like Wonder Woman with bulletproof bracelets, you'll be bounced out of this pursuit dejected.

**Comfortable going it alone, but amiable in social situations.** This is an odd combination, but a necessary one for any kind of journalist. A travel writer, especially a guidebook or feature writer, is often traveling alone, eating meals alone, staying in hotel rooms alone, riding planes and buses alone. There's nobody to bounce ideas off of in the room. On the other hand, the writer must be regularly starting up conversations with complete strangers: digging for information, getting quotes, asking for other contacts, finding out how things work, and getting others' opinions. The only writers who don't need these dual qualities are ones whose entire writing output comes out of group press trips. (Unfortunately though, it's rare that one of those people turns in consistently great work that is refreshing or surprising.)

**Observant.** Do you know how many different kinds of birds are singing outside your window? Do you notice what music is playing when you enter a restaurant or hotel? Blindfolded, can you taste the difference between Chardonnay and Sauvignon Blanc, between Pilsner and Pale Ale, between Ethiopian coffee and Sumatran coffee, between Thai food and Vietnamese food? Can you tell the differences just from the aromas? Can you describe a Chihuahua to a blind person? Do you notice the characteristics of the other diners in the café where you're having coffee? Can you describe the scene in the town square where you are sitting in such a way on paper that I see the details in my mind?

Most of these skills are developed, not innate, but it's hard to be a great writer without them.

**Curious.** This may be the most important quality of all, but it's one that seldom gets discussed because this one *does* need to be innate. If you are a closed-minded, dogmatic person who only gets news from one source, doesn't have a passport, and never reads quality fiction, you are going to be a lousy travel writer. Sure, that's my opinion, but it's based on close to two decades of experience meeting hundreds of other travel writers. All the good ones are open-minded and very curious about the world, about other peoples' opinions, about other cultures and religions.

As a travel writer you are constantly diving into subjects you previously knew nothing about. If you can't investigate these stories and places with an open heart and mind, it's nearly impossible to do a good job and it will show. Being a stubborn pundit with rigid beliefs works fine if you're a political columnist, but it's toxic for a travel reporter.

**Passionate.** Every good travel writer I know is passionate about travel, just as every food writer I know is passionate about cooking. You don't see someone who seldom watches sports become a sports writer. I'd rather get poked in the eye with a knitting needle than to write about crafts, so of course I'll never cover that subject. If you think it would be fun to be a travel writer because you had a great time on your last vacation—which was three years ago—this is probably not the right subject for you. If you haven't gotten away every chance you had, travel is not your passion. Become a mommy blogger, a music reviewer, or a gardening writer instead.

Before going down any of the various paths available to writers, it's important to reflect on whether travel itself is truly a subject that gets you excited. Not the highlights of a great vacation, but the entire experience: the bus journey, the strange food, different languages, finding your way in a foreign land.

Just as an artist becomes a painter for reasons other than the associated income, the tough slog of becoming a successful travel writer requires an above-average level of interest in the subject. Be sure too that you have the skills and tenacity to turn this passion into income. As a business writer friend of mine likes to say, just because you love to drink doesn't mean you should own a bar.

*If someone dear to me wanted to become a travel writer, I would advise that they look deeply and see if it is really their passion. Contrary to what the travel writing schools advertise about earning six figures a year, doing it for the money alone is a sure way to fail. If it is your love and passion push ahead!*

– John Lamkin, freelance travel writer and photographer

# Traditional Earning Opportunities as a Travel Writer

While this book may be called "Travel Writing 2.0," the rise of one media does not mean the automatic fall of another. More than half the travel writers I contacted for this book are still making at the majority of their income from print. To ignore these outlets, especially considering their still-higher pay, would put this book at least three years ahead of its time. For now, we're still in a transition phase. The day I finished up the draft of this book, I sent out a $500 ad invoice for one of my websites, but then signed and faxed a $1,000 contract for a magazine story. I'm not turning my back on print just yet.

As some of the examples in the previous chapter illustrate, few freelance travel writers are one-trick ponies. Though most have a defined niche, which is incredibly important in terms of standing out from the pack, they have multiple income streams deriving from different kinds of work. Here's the bio for one of them I know well:

Christopher Elliott is *National Geographic Traveler* magazine's reader advocate and writes the syndicated *Travel Troubleshooter* column, which appears in more than 50 U.S. newspapers and Web sites. He produces a popular weekly commentary and podcast on MSNBC.com and writes the *Navigator* column in Sunday's *Washington Post*. He is also editor of the Elliott.org blog and one of the two editors of ConsumerTraveler.com.

Christopher will often spin one subject three or four different ways to put it in three or four different outlets, some owned by him, some by others. This is how many successful writers turn one trip or idea into a whole portfolio of articles.

Writers like Tim Cahill and Pico Iyer have done well taking features they wrote for magazines and packaging them as chapters in a book.

Some magazine feature writers are able to take one trip sponsored by one magazine and get paid enough to justify all the time spent on that trip, but this is rare. Most writers need to hustle more than this, turning each trip into multiple stories.

Here's an example of how that works when it works well. A few years back I took my first trip to Peru and spent two and a half weeks on the ground. Even though my wife was with me and I was in vacation mode part of the time, here's what eventually came out of that trip over the course of several years:

1) 28 hotel reviews for a trade publication
2) 9 hotel reviews for LuxuryLatinAmerica.com
3) "Through the Eyes of a Porter" article for *South American Explorer* magazine
4) A different slant on the porter article for *International Travel News*
5) "Saving Machu Picchu" for *Transitions Abroad* (when it was a print magazine)
6) "The Coca Plant Paradox" for *Transitions Abroad*
7) A front-page destination story for the *St. Petersburg Times* newspaper
8) "On the Pisco Trail in Peru" feature story for *Imbibe* magazine
9) "Inca Trail 101" for Backcountry.com's web magazine
10) "Slow Roads to Machu Picchu" in the *Boston Globe* (with added material from a second trip later)
11) Multiple Peru posts on the Cheapest Destinations blog
12) Chapter updates for *The World's Cheapest Destinations*

Now granted, not every trip generates a few grand in income like this one did and if I hadn't spent sufficient time there traveling independently, half of this would never have come to pass. That's one disadvantage of press trips, which we'll cover later: you don't control your time or schedule and these trips are often too short, too frantic, or both.

I've had a similar output on several other trips, however, with articles continuing to trickle out years after I left the place. I've placed articles from a two-week trip to Hungary and the Czech Republic in around a dozen outlets as well, from a hotel website to a drinks magazines to a blog run by a tour company. Some of them were pure service pieces, others were damn fine narratives if I may say so myself. I never wrote some editor or tourism person saying, "I want to do a story about Hungary." Instead my pitches centered around the history of Hungarian wine and the biking greenways of Moravia. These were commercially viable but unusual and they lent themselves to branching off in multiple directions for different outlets, print and online. My revenue flowed from many taps, some print, some online.

In this section I'll break down the different revenue streams coming from traditional outlets and explain how to go about earning income in those areas.

# Magazine Print Writing

This is what most people daydream about when they say, "I want to be a travel writer." You jet off to some far-flung place on a fat expense account, write up a story on the fabulous time you had there while lounging around the pool, then open your mailbox soon after to find a four-figure check in an envelope. Ah, the life.

Unfortunately, living that scenario on a regular basis and making a great income from this work alone is incredibly rare—the equivalent of being drafted into the NBA or England's Premier League. For every long feature story in a major travel magazine, there are a thousand short little articles that make up the bulk of a writer's work. After all, even if you are successful enough to manage to net an average of $2,000 per feature, getting one of those plumb assignments every month will only earn you $24,000 a year before taxes. Let's even assume you get assigned longer pieces or a double now and then and it averages out to $3,000 per month, or $36,000 per year before taxes. If you live in New York City or London, good luck living off that.

So most freelance writers try to land as many assignments as they can from as many outlets as they can, hoping it all adds up to a decent income over time. It's not unusual for a busy freelancer to be juggling interviews and research for five assignments at once, writing until midnight on one article after checking out the city sights and hotels all day for another. The only freelance writers who can manage that stereotype of sipping piña coladas by the resort pool while "on assignment" are those who have someone else actually paying the bills at home. Or they are retired.

It's hard to generalize about print pay rates because they are really all over the map. Big famous magazines that everyone has heard of will pay $1 to $2 per word, sometimes a bit more for the right high-profile writer. There's a tier of quality magazines, top newspapers, and trades after that paying a bit less, then there's another tier of regional magazines and smaller circulation pubs that get into the 10 cents to 25 cents range. The local equivalent of that $1 to $2 per word range is rare in Canada, the UK, and Australia, partly because of lower potential circulation—and advertising. In all countries there is then a whole range of barely-hanging-on magazines and newspapers that pay you a pittance, assuming you manage to actually get paid.

Some publications will openly list their pay scales in guidelines or in reference book listings. Others treat them like a secret handshake, only revealing them when they give you an assignment. In those cases it may be open to negotiation, but only if you have any real leverage on your side.

Now that we have that out of the way, assuming you still want to pursue this route, here are the steps.

1) Come up with a unique angle that is perfect for a specific publication's style and content

2) Send a pitch e-mail (a query letter) showing you know the publication well, why this ideas is right for them, and why you are the person to write this piece.
3) If you get rejected, go back to number 1. Re-slant the pitch and try elsewhere. If your idea gets accepted, get the terms in writing and go to work. (They may pay expenses, but often will not, so keep the ideas focused on places you can get to easily or are already visiting.)
4) Study the publication again as you are writing and make sure your content, style, and tone fit in well with what's already there.
5) After multiple drafts and polishing edits, turn in your story on time or early.
6) Make any requested changes or follow up after a reasonable time to see if any other edits are needed.
7) Eventually get paid.
8) If possible, see if this trip or research can be applied to other articles. Pitch those to different publications.
9) Pitch the editor with another idea while he/she still remembers who you are.

This is the way it has been done for generations, though at least e-mail has sped up the rejection process. It hasn't made most editors any faster or more considerate, however, so you'll still do lots of waiting and you'll still encounter plenty of "pocket vetoes" where the harried editor never gets around to responding to you. (This still drives me crazy, by the way, and I've been dealing with it since the days of mailing completed stories and slides by post from Bangkok. As an editor, I personally respond to every query.)

You need *lots* of patience for this path.

There are entire books written just on the query part of this process—overkill if you ask the editor in me—and I've listed some of them in the resources section. Obviously I've just simplified this process to the bare essence. You can learn plenty more on this subject by reading other books, visiting writing websites listed in the resources, and hanging out in the right forums. But sooner or later you just have to get out there and get bloodied.

Here are some factors that will help your odds.

## *Develop a portfolio*

Like many editors, when I get a pitch from a writer, I look first at their credentials, second at their idea. I know a terrific writer can make almost anything sound interesting, while a bad writer can take the greatest trip in the world and turn it into a dead-boring story. I want to see what you've written already to see if you and your style are a good match. I want to know your area(s) of expertise. This matters far more than what you've put into your query letter. Other editors feel differently, but better safe than sorry on the way you project your image.

So develop a portfolio of articles before you go pitching to the big boys. These days there's not such a stigma about articles written for the web as there was when I started doing online articles more than a decade ago. So get in where you can, print or web, and start writing unique things that are worth noticing. Then put up a portfolio page that only requires a link in your pitch to see what you've accomplished. (In cases where the article only appeared in print, you can convert it to a PDF that can be opened in a browser.)

In theory you could limp along without this by linking to your blog, your LinkedIn site, or some other substitute, but I wouldn't advise it. You may get a cranky editor like me who thinks, "If this person can't be bothered to create a portfolio, how hard are they going to work on this article they're pitching?" Turn off the social media streams for a while and go make something built to last.

You can set up a portfolio site using simple "what you see is what you get" (WYSIWYG) templates without having to know any HTML. You can do this through the likes of Web.com, GoDaddy.com, Bravenet.com and others, but if I were doing this tomorrow I would probably go with iPage.com. They're only $3.50 a month and they throw in a lot for that amount.

See examples of good sites and more on this subject in the Next Steps to Success section.

## *Really study the publication you're pitching to*

Whether your target publication is print, digital, broadcast, or sent by a medium that hasn't been invented yet, this part is *extremely* important. Most magazines and webzines publish writers' guidelines somewhere: on their website, in the Writer's Marketplace book, in the Wooden Horse database, or elsewhere. Nearly every set of guidelines will tell you to study past issues and articles to see what works for their publication. (Even if they don't publish guidelines, assume this is a requirement. )

As any editor will tell you, however, far too many writers ignore this advice and send terrible, badly targeted queries. Now that I'm an editor myself, I'm flabbergasted at some of the awful pitches I get that have nothing to do with what Perceptive Travel is about. In some cases it is obvious they have sent the same pitch to dozens of editors at once, hoping some fool will bite. (In a few cases they've even blasted it out to 50 editors at once, putting all of them in the "To" field.) There's no excuse for this and if you start off on the wrong foot with an editor, you will probably never get a second chance. If I get two dud pitches in a row from a writer, no way I'm ever going to open a third. Instant delete. That may sound harsh, but others won't even give you that much latitude.

Before ever querying a publication, *really* study what they are about. For print, dissect at least the current issue, but preferably a few issues if you can

> *The good writers know our site and they submit ideas that fit our needs. They look at our index of articles, see missing topics and then fill those. We don't like people who send us 'I've always loved to travel and now I'm going on a trip to Nepal and I'd really love to write about it for you.' We get lots of those. None of them get assignments.*
>
> – Janna Graber
> Executive Director of
> GoWorldTravel.com and
> GoColorado.com.

find them in a library or can access them online. Read the letter from the editor. Study the table of contents. Figure out which section of the magazine is right for your idea. Get an idea of word counts, writing style, point of view, and tense—the mechanics of the publication. Look at the story array, travel budgets in the sidebars, and what kinds of ads are there to get a sense of the target audience. If they have a media kit on their site, sometimes posted under "Advertise with us," then study that to see how the magazine wants to be perceived. If you're lucky there will even be an editorial schedule there for coming issues. (If not, a subscription to the Wooden Horse database will get it for you if it's available.)

"Gosh Tim, that's a lot of work," you may be thinking. "Why would I do all that for an idea they probably won't accept?"

Well, do you want your chance of success to be 5 percent or…zero? If you don't take the time to match your slant to the publication, you have almost no chance of getting an assignment. Go bet on some horses because your odds will be better.

There are some short cuts out there that will help this process even more, like the pitching tips available to paid Avant Guild members at MediaBistro.com. Follow the advice to the letter when it comes from the editor's mouth. Craft your query with specific references to the publication—showing you've done your homework—and make the subject line relevant to your idea. After all this, you'll at least have a shot at getting noticed. Ignore these steps and your query will be lucky to even get a form letter rejection.

Some people who do all this correctly may get a great break right away—it can be done. Sheila Scarborough's first real travel piece was in a major publication. She says she did it "by reading a bunch of books on freelance writing, paying careful attention to the content of magazines that I subscribed to, and pitching a story to *National Geographic Traveler* that I thought might fit based on reading the magazine for years. It worked."

## Aim appropriately

As I mentioned earlier, there are certain rules in place for print magazines, more of them than with the less structured web. Only the very smallest will hire you to do a feature story unless you a) have a fantastic track record b) know the editor well or c) are the indisputable go-to expert on that subject. Otherwise you need to pay your dues and break in with something smaller. An editor will typically give you a few small assignments of 200 to 400 words first to see if you are dependable and can conform well to their style. It gives the appearance of meritocracy, but it's really not. Even if you've done five major features for magazine A, the editor of magazine B still probably won't assign you a big feature if she hasn't worked with you. Relationships matter a lot.

So if you keep trying to hit a home run without ever getting a base hit, you will get very frustrated. Start off sending queries to smaller publications that hire lots of freelancers before you even think about querying fortresses like *Travel & Leisure* or the *New York Times*. Otherwise it's the equivalent of wanting to try out for the Yankees without ever playing in the minor leagues. You are wasting your time and that of an editor—who will not appreciate it in the least. If a big glossy is going to assign a short piece to an inexperienced writer, they'll just give it to one of their junior editors or interns and do it in house. They don't need a freelancer for that.

Even when you are pitching those smaller publications, think small and focused. For every big feature story in a magazine there are at least 20 to 40 pieces taking up a page or less. Unless you are a masochist, go for where the work is and come up with bite-sized story ideas that can be explained in a paragraph and will run only a few paragraphs more in print. Like it or not, this is what most editors really need from you. And editors are your customers in the print world. If they don't want to buy what you're selling, you will not get any assignments.

Thinking about the what the editors are buying and publishing regularly is important too. Most of the glossy travel mags really sell themselves to advertisers as "lifestyle publications," which is why they are filled with ads for luxury cars, jewelry, watches, and perfume. Flip through them month after month and you'll notice that the pretty pictures are what matter the most. Often the words seem to be there merely to be an accessory to the photographs. At least half the contributor credits in the front of the publication are usually photographers, not writers. The magazines are selling a fantasy world and that world does not include grotty destinations that are really hard to reach. It does not include huts in the woods and days without showers. Other magazines' readers eat that stuff up, so go pitch to them instead.

Once you target correctly and actually get an assignment, don't pop the bubbly until you've got something in writing—preferably a contract, but at the least an e-mail spelling out the terms on pay, deadline, and rights. The scope of all that will put you to sleep if I cover it here, but these are the things you want to be concerned about:

- How much you'll get paid
- When you'll get paid
- What is required of you (word count, photos, specific information to be included)
- The deadline
- Who owns the various rights to text and photos
- What happens if they don't use the story (a "kill fee" promises you a percentage of the pay if they don't use the article.)

The best publications pay "on acceptance," which means when they accept the article they send you money, or they at least send it prior to publication. More common is for you to get paid "upon publication" or "x weeks after publication." This is the main reason why the idea of trying to support yourself as a travel writer when you set off on a round-the-world trip is pure fantasy for a new writer. If you're writing for print, most of the checks won't arrive until after your journey is finished and you're back home. In some cases, they don't arrive at all—the magazine goes under before you get paid.

For the rights part, ideally you want to keep the rights to what you produce so you can resell the stories elsewhere, but I personally don't care about this as much as some writers do. If it's "work for hire," meaning the publication owns all the rights, I just adjust my effort accordingly. For example I'll make sure I'm not sending something that I'd be duplicating elsewhere or sending my best photos. For a hotel review, for example, they can have the rights to my prose and pictures if they pay is appropriate. I'll be on to something else and probably wouldn't sell that review elsewhere anyway.

If you're a prolific writer and photographer with lots of assignments, rights aren't such a big deal. But if you've put together a masterpiece that's unique and you could conceivably resell it to multiple outlets (or use it later as a chapter in a book), you don't want to give up all the rights.

If you're principally a photographer, you probably don't want to give up *any* of your photo rights unless you're being paid handsomely for it. So you want to sell "First North American Rights," "First Electronic Rights" (often with a certain exclusion period), or something else that's restricted to a single instance. "All Rights" means they can do whatever they want with it in any media for eternity.

Once all that is worked out, do a great job. Make your first assignment as fantastic as it can possibly be. Edit, proof, and then edit some more. Have at least one other person edit it again. Then hand it in early, exactly as requested. Make any changes requested and furnish any additional information requested with a smile.

When you eventually get that paycheck, now it's time to celebrate. Parlay that article into more assignments. Then do it all again.

# Newspaper Writing

This type of media is in trouble, no doubt. There's one advantage to new writers when it comes to newspapers though: the editors aren't as hung up on your track record.

"In the United States, newspaper travel editors don't want to receive queries for stories; they want to get the already written story for them to consider," says David Farley, an author who teaches travel writing classes at New York University. "This is good news for newbies: it means you don't have to have a list of already published clips to show off with your query. Instead, you can just send in the finished piece and the editor will consider it by the piece's own merits and not necessarily what you've published (or haven't published) in the past. This is how I first broke into travel writing. I submitted a story on Rome to the *Chicago Tribune* travel section and they published it. After I established a working relationship with the editor, I could then start pitching."

Unfortunately, the *Chicago Tribune* is one of the few papers that still has a viable travel section on Sundays. Many of the others are now just collections of wire service stories with maybe one feature written by a staffer who went on a press trip. My own lame paper in a city of one million people has a single page of travel stories most weekends, none of them written by anyone in the area. *USA Today* has a good weekly travel section, but it is almost all staff-written. Travel stories in the *Wall Street Journal* are mostly written by regular columnists or those working in a foreign office as a news reporter. Breaking into the *New York Times* is almost as tough as bagging a feature in a major magazine, with the added annoyance that they have lower pay and what may be the most restrictive freelance contract on Earth.

In 2010 there were fewer than 20 full-time travel editors at U.S. newspapers and I wouldn't be surprised if there are 12 by the time you read this book. That doesn't mean other papers don't accept travel stories, but there are fewer slots to fill each year. By 2015 we could be sliding toward a future with seven decent U.S. newspaper travel sections and that's it: the five largest cities plus two national papers. Do your homework and aim carefully.

The U.K. and some other countries are certainly faring better than the U.S., so maybe there's another 10 years left in the system there, but the future doesn't look bright. If appearing in a newspaper travel section is one of your life goals, you had better get on that pronto.

As David Farley mentioned, most newspaper editors don't want to see queries. Send them a finished piece or send the first two or three paragraphs of it—that's usually all they're going to read before making their decision anyway. Newspaper editors know what they want and they can tell in a flash if you've got what it takes to meet their requirements. If your piece is not in AP style, if there are typos, or if you take too long to get to the point, you're out in five seconds flat.

Many newspapers still cling to a "no sponsored trips" policy, but then lower their pay rates each year, adding insult to injury. Plus the pay was already pretty crappy before. To be frank, this is the most dead-end option in this chapter. If you are a religious person, put newspapers in your prayers because we really need for them to stick around if we want to keep getting relevant local news and investigative reporting. Unfortunately, they're already last century's news when it comes to travel.

# Writing for Trades

Business to business magazines are more stable than consumer ones because they have a more predictable readership and revenue stream. Whether it's mining or footwear or travel, the readers are people who live and breathe that business. The advertisers are companies who want, or must, reach those readers and create a favorable impression. With many trade magazines, there's no such thing as a "Chinese Wall" between editorial and advertising either: you spend a lot of money on advertising and the editorial coverage will follow.

So writing for the trades can be a more lucrative and dependable pursuit if you can get your foot in and then deliver on a regular basis. There are travel trade magazines like *Travel Weekly, Meetings & Conventions, Hotel & Motel Management*, and *Travel Agent*. There are also online-only publications, plus some others that are sold by subscription only to travel agents, such as *Star Service Online* (reviews of top hotels) and *Weissmann Reports* (in-depth destination guides).

Ironically, there is often less competition for slots in these publications as there is for consumer magazines because most writers don't take the time to research them, you won't find them on newsstands, and there's no glory in it—often you don't even get a byline. Writing for the trades is much less of a roller coaster though and if you get in good with one of them, you can probably parlay that into assignments from others run by the same company. Two publishers in particular—Northstar and Questex—have the majority of the big travel trade imprints.

> *At first I wanted the high profile bylines in magazines and newspapers. Now I'm going where the paychecks are, and increasingly that's working for companies/corporations: blogging and writing for websites, as well as print custom publishing (i.e. brochures for tourist boards or travel agent magazines). It's not strict travel editorial, for sure, but I still consider myself a "travel writer." I envision continuing the same mix of income streams I have now: a combo of print editorial and custom advertorial or corporate gigs.*
>
> – Kara Williams, freelance writer and blogger

Pitching to the trades is more of a pull than a push. Your goal is to get an assignment, not to sell them on your idea. They have their own very clear ideas about what they need and the best bet for success here is to meet those needs competently and on time. Obtain a copy of their writer's guidelines and editorial calendar by calling the editorial office if they are not published online. When you approach the editor, your letter should focus on where you live (for local assignments), where you'll be traveling in the next six months or year, and your qualifications. They may want to see your résumé/c.v. as well, so have one ready in case.

# Guidebook Writing

Guidebook writing is as much about researching, project management, and time management as it is about actual writing and the day-to-day job is frequently far from glamorous. As the guidebook competition has increased, pay has decreased. To make the numbers work, most new writers have to work 12-hour days for weeks on end, researching all day and writing much of the night. After all that they are lucky to earn more than minimum wage after expenses and they wake up one day wondering what happened to the last three months of their life.

In the good ole days these guidebook writers received royalties on top of their fee payment, so the writers who did successive editions could end up with a nice ongoing income stream. Those contracts are getting rare, however, and most publishers now do some kind of straight "work for hire" agreement with expected expenses rolled into the total amount.

The day-to-day work involves inspecting dozens of hotels and restaurants in each location, taking down bus and train schedule times, getting opening hours for every notable museum and attraction, figuring out prices for everything, all while also trying to formulate a description of the place that doesn't sound like what everyone else has already written. Some of the better publishers furnish expenses in addition to the book advance, but others just lump it all together. Either way you will not be living the high life. Most writers either rent an apartment to have a home base or they stay in cheap hotels on the move. They rarely get to eat leisurely meals at all the fancy restaurants they are including or stay at all the luxury hotels listed in the guide. Some do get hosted along the way, but in other cases this is prohibited by the publisher.

> *It is rarely possible to visit more than five or six restaurants and four or five hotels. Those numbers go way down if you do, in fact, visit any of the sites the town is known for. The numbers go down if transportation is delayed, the weather sucks, you don't feel well, or any of the other thousand disruptions that are bound to surface in international travel. Then there's the whole issue of trying to review nightlife, already wiped out from a day's work, with the full knowledge that the next morning you have to get up and start all over again.*
>
> *- Thomas Kohnstamm in Do Travel Writers Go to Hell?*

I've never written a guidebook. It's a monumental job and frankly it scares me. I've gotten a taste of what's required when doing the Weissmann Travel Reports—trade publications used by travel agents for their clients. After a week solid of checking phone numbers, bus schedules, and restaurant hours, I'm exhausted. Writing a guidebook is very hard work. It's the toughest job in travel writing and most people who think they want to do it have no earthly idea of how draining and time-sucking it can turn out to be.

One of the most prolific writers I know is Lara Dunston, whose name graces dozens of guidebooks and a steady stream of magazine features she finds time to fire off before she moves on to a new place. "I co-author with my husband and he's also a photographer so we pitch and sell our work as a package. We're doing rather nicely, although working incredibly hard to derive the income we're making. We work seven days a week and we only really take a few hours off at Christmas."

Some writers do make good money doing mostly guidebook work, but usually these are writers who are getting royalties from a successful guide they have researched for several editions. Or they are writers like Dunston who cram many projects into a year and work their guidebook research into major feature stories for magazines as well. After a while though, this grind can wear you out, especially if you see your earnings per project declining. David Stanley, who has put out dozens of guidebooks with his name on the cover, has this to say now: "I may give up working on print guidebooks entirely and focus exclusively on the web."

For new writers, however, a guidebook glut and low pay have combined to make guidebook writing jobs some of the easiest ones to land.

*Write stories for travel websites and your local weekly newspapers, for free if need be. In the meantime, study publishing, and the travel market. Pay attention to the quality of writing. And of course, take a long, research-oriented vacation in the region you'd like to cover. Finally, collect your clips, write a great bio, and send your pitch to the publishers who may need a book, or articles, about the region. Not exactly groundbreaking advice, but I think a lot of people who could be great travel writers simply never get around to pitching the book.*

*- Paige Penland, guidebook author and freelance writer*

When there were only a few guidebook companies out there, they seldom had to advertise openings or hire new writers to work for them. The cream of the crop wanted those assignments. Now that there are so many guides out there and veterans have wizened up to the low pay scales, it's easier than ever to find open assignments. See the resources section at the end for where to look for these but be warned: it will not be a pretty picture when you realistically estimate the research time and expenses then look at what you will be paid. Go in prepared to be poor for a while.

Here's my advice to alleviate some of that: make your first guidebook assignment one for your own city or state. You won't spend so much on travel expenses, you'll already know much of the area, and you can do it all faster because you know where to look for information. Keep track of your hours so you'll know how long it all took, including edits and template inputs. Then when it comes time to evaluate the next possible assignment, you can just double the time and expenses to get an idea of whether the job is worth taking.

Guidebook writing can be rewarding work for the right kind of person, but make sure you *are* the right kind of person. Ideally, you are super organized, obsessive about getting the facts straight, detail-oriented, good at time management, and very responsible. If you're a big picture creative type who delights in creating beautiful prose, don't take a guidebook job. Both you and your editor will be miserable before it's all over.

Here's what Brice Gosnell, the person responsible for hiring writers at Lonely Planet has to say about what's important to them.

*We need people who are able to write well, of course, because it means more editing time for us if they cannot. It's not about flowery language though; we need a journalistic approach, seeing a place or situation from all sides. We will include controversial things, but we strive to provide balance. Even more important, however, is being travel savvy. We want someone who is well-traveled, not someone who just took their first trip out of college. When we look at a writer's potential, their travel history comes first.*

*Expertise and experience in a specific area is very important for who we hire. If you know an area well already, you have an advantage. Also, everyone wants to write about Paris. We need someone who wants to write about Kazakhstan or Suriname. If you can identify yourself as someone who wants to go to the lesser-known spots, great. Knowing another language is a great advantage. Having a special expertise in something gives you a definite advantage too—say a degree in art history. In a case like that we may hire you for a special section. We might go to you for the artwork part, to make it more interesting, to connect the dots.*

*On the ground, we want you to be observant, to give us those special moments, those things that nobody else would know. Tell us what's special to do apart from what the crowds are doing. Give us insider tips. Also, be open to feedback, which is often much harder for young writers. Remember, we are giving you feedback because we want to keep working with you. Don't ask a million and 20 questions by e-mail and annoy your editors to death. Pick up the phone and have a conversation when you need an answer that's not in your guidelines—it's far faster.*

- Brice Gosnell, Publisher for the Americas, Lonely Planet

Gosnell wants to stress to writers that the Lonely Planet empire is not an impenetrable fortress, that with the volume of publications they are releasing, they are always looking for talented new writers. "Call us with an idea. If it looks like a promising match, we'll set up a meeting. We've clearly identified what we need and know what to expect, so we tend to move quickly on hiring decisions."

Joshua Berman has written a variety of Moon Handbook guides. He got his big break after working for the Peace Corps in Nicaragua. "My coauthor and I pitched our first guidebook to Moon. We told them we were going to write the first ever comprehensive guide to Nicaragua and we wanted to do it for them. They gave us the job, then a few years later, offered me Belize when that writer retired." Later Berman also got tapped to write *Living Abroad in Nicaragua*.

In my conversation with Gosnell, he stressed that Lonely Planet pays according to what the book requires rather than by it will probably earn or on some formula based on a flat fee. In other words, you get paid more for covering the Galapagos or Bhutan than you do to write a book about Guatemala. Since they require you to physically visit every place covered in the book, your expected travel expenses are a part of the equation.

With many other publishers, you are offered a flat fee that does not take any of this into account and you are on your own to make it work. So naturally, writers cut corners and find ways to research places remotely. (Remember that next time your guidebook leads you astray and choose accordingly in the future.) I'm not going to incur the wrath of publishers here by saying who pays terribly and who doesn't, but

> The last few years have completely changed the way writing and photography are marketed, with so much digital content coming out. Success is going to be very slippery in this context.
>
> – Michael Buckley is, guidebook author for Bradt and Moon Handbooks.

72

for overall working conditions, I've met very few authors who have bad things to say about working for Lonely Planet or Moon/Avalon. Other writers have had great experiences with each of the other guidebook companies as well. Some pay more, some less. Some are hungry for new writers; others tend to use a pool of people they trust. Research and apply to find out.

This is one of the few areas of travel writing where you can actually apply for a gig and get it. Nose around on the websites of the various guidebook companies and you will often find a section outlining parts of the world where there are seeking writers to fill a hole. You may find, for example, that they need someone to update a Buenos Aires guide, write the first edition of their Manitoba guide, and write the southeast section for their USA guide. If you don't see a section like that, you will at least usually find contact information for submitting a work history or proposal.

This is how Zora O'Neill got her start in travel writing. "I answered an ad! Really! I'd been trying to get into travel writing for magazines, but a friend forwarded an ad from Moon guides, about the new (at that time) Metro series and the New York guide they were hiring for. I was assigned to write the hotels section. I used that to approach other guidebook publishers and it snowballed." Now Zora has written more guides for Moon plus others for Lonely Planet and Rough Guides, on destinations from Amsterdam to Santa Fe, from Mexico to Egypt. She also got a cookbook published in the process: *Forking Fantastic!*

If you apply and eventually get assigned to cover a certain area, take a good look at the contract and carefully calculate your expected expenses. No matter how good it sounds otherwise, accepting a book contract that will take months out of your life but won't even cover your expenses on the road is probably going to make you resentful unless you have good motives for putting up with this. Many a guidebook writer has accepted unfavorable terms just to break in and get the experience. As long as they knew this going in, they were able to retain a positive attitude.

Those who have signed on without doing any calculations have found halfway through that they were going to come out poorer on the other end of the assignment than they were going in. Sometimes they get angry and get sloppy, they start cutting corners, and the guidebook is not as sharp as it should be. The writer is unhappy and is soured on the experience. The editor is unhappy and never wants to hire that writer again. The readers of the guidebook are unhappy because there are holes and mistakes that mess up their trip. Nobody wins.

*In a guidebook writer I look for a love of the place and a genuine enthusiasm to share knowledge to make travelers' experiences more valuable. This is key because without that as the foundation, it's hard to get through as grueling a project as writing a travel guide. I also look for people who can think strategically—it's a good sign when this comes out when I haven't even asked the question yet. Finally, I look for people who respond well to feedback and suggestions. That's not to say I expect all authors to do everything I want. I feel like the best authors are the ones where we're on the same wavelength most of the time, but they speak up when they don't agree with something.*

- Grace Fujimoto, acquisitions director at Avalon Travel (Moon Handbooks and Dog Lover's Companion series).

# Book Writing

"You should write a book!"

Nearly everyone who has traveled around the world for a year has heard this from at least one of their well-meaning friends or relatives. Maybe from all of them. They say this because they can't fathom that tens of thousands of people are traveling around the world right this minute and that it's really not a very unique experience anymore. Most also don't understand that writers make very little money from book sales.

I got confronted with this reality early, as a young child when we picked up a friend of my mom's one day in the car. She was a children's book author and I had four of her titles, autographed, on a shelf in my bedroom. I couldn't believe it when we got there: she lived in a vine-covered little house with peeling paint on a rutted dirt road. Her rusty car, which was waiting to be towed to the shop for repairs, sat in the driveway. During a conversation in the car it came out that she didn't even have a TV. None of this made sense to me. When I eventually had my mother alone, I asked why her friend didn't live in a big fancy house. Why wasn't she rich? "She's not world famous," my mom replied with a laugh. "She just writes nature books for kids. It's what she enjoys doing."

For the vast majority of authors, writing a book has never resulted in much of a payoff. The book distribution business has never been logical and there are too many efficiency leaks in the system for any one party to really do well. The bookstore chains are in big trouble (sales declining 5-10% every year), the publishers are in big trouble (cutting staff, reducing the number of imprints), and author advances keep declining or disappearing completely except for a few high-profile authors who are a sure bet.

This is not a problem unique to travel writers, of course. Many famous writers were working day jobs for four or five books before they started making writing their full-time job. Faulkner was a postmaster. William S. Burroughs was a copywriter. T.S. Eliot was a bank clerk. Nicholas Sparks sold pharmaceutical products. In an article in *Poets & Writers*, a group of literary agents guessed that no more than 100 American novelists support themselves from their writing alone.

Amazon has been a godsend for many authors, giving life to books that wouldn't have found much action in a physical bookstore, and for print-on-demand (P.O.D.) or other forms of self-published books, this has meant the difference between selling to a few relatives to selling to thousands of strangers. By being 10 times more efficient than the traditional system—not a hard thing to achieve really—Amazon has changed the game. Bookstores hate this and publishers aren't at all happy about the power Amazon wields, but for authors the rise of online sales has been a beautiful thing. With Apple's introduction of the iPad and other readers making inroads, competition is heating up as well.

We are in a transition phase though, as in many other industries moving from a physical product to a digital one. As the music business found and the movie industry is starting to find, it's hard to charge as much for digital goods as physical ones. Some publishers have embraced the difference and made it a wash by saving money in other areas, such as paper and shipping costs. Some have turned to efficient print-on-demand systems so there are no books printed that will later have to be destroyed as returns.

The obvious end step would be a world where we are all reading books on some kind of digital reader. Just as we will not suddenly see an end to CDs or DVDs, however (or even vinyl), this will not be a 100% transformation. It could be a decade before e-book readers become mainstream. Plenty of people who don't travel much are perfectly happy with the current form: a book is inexpensive and there's no recharging necessary. You have a huge selection at the library for free.

That isn't stopping lots of companies from jumping in with both feet, however. First there was the Sony Reader and the Amazon Kindle, and then a competing one called Nook from Barnes & Noble. Seven more were introduced at the 2010 Consumer Electronics show, with names like Que, Skiff, eDGe, and Copia. Then the iPad. You can bet more readers, slates, and pads will come out each year until the clear winners emerge.

For now, the digital reading experience isn't close to what it could be, so it is still a niche in the market. The general population still isn't happy with the price, first of all, since a reader typically costs as much as 10 hardcover books—before you even load it with books. Illustrations don't render well, the Kindle is black-and-white only, and so far even the iPad can't give you the coffee table book experience with lots of large color photos. An electronic gadget is still not as pleasant to hold in bed or in a hammock as a book. You can't take them to places with no electricity for very long. Plus there's the inherent flaw that there's no such thing as a "used book" in the digital world and the devices discourage sharing. You pay full price or you don't read it. Great for publishers and authors, but not so great for readers used to loaning, sharing, yard sale buying, and checking things out from libraries.

For authors going through the traditional system, electronic books are a wash at best. Unless people suddenly start buying lots more books overall, there's not going to be any more money than before in the author's royalty check—maybe even less since the list price is lower.

For many writers, the reason to write a book goes beyond the bottom line though. For one thing, you can say and do a lot more in a book than you can in any commercial travel article. Here's how Chuck Thompson put it in *Smile While You're Lying*:

"The stories my friends actually pay attention to never seem to interest editors, most of them emasculated by demands to portray travel as an unbroken fantasy of on-time departures, courteous flunkies, sugar-white beaches, fascinating cities, charming locals, first-class hotels, golden days, purple nights, and, of course, 'an exotic blend of the ancient and the modern.'"

When you write a book, you've got many pages to give good travel stories their due. You don't have to worry that an editor will strike something because it will annoy an advertiser, that it's "too negative." Quite the opposite actually: books about disasters and trips gone wrong sell as well or sometimes better than fantasy fulfillment books that get picked up by book clubs. (For one thing, they sell to both sexes.) Bad trips are bankable.

The main reason to write a book, however, is it still transcends every other form of printed media and gives you an air of credibility that's hard to match in other ways. Your grandma might not know what a blog is and your 12-year-old cousin thinks having a blog is about as noteworthy as having a cell phone. Both will be impressed if you put a book with your name on it in their hand, however.

> *I'm in the midst of a transition and I'd like to focus more on book projects instead of periodical or online articles. This means less income in the short term, but hopefully a better platform for more travel writing in the future. My first two books—*Vagabonding *and* Marco Polo Didn't Go There— *have been a great platform for my career, and I believe that books (more than articles) have more staying power in taking your career to a new level.*
>
> *I realize this isn't in keeping with the new media landscape, which is skewing even more towards online media— and even video—but I think that in-depth, well-written and researched projects (like books) have a way of standing out, regardless of whatever new media becomes fashionable.*
>
> - Rolf Potts, author and writer

## How Book Authors Make Money

Let's step back though and look at the general structure of payments. Writing a book and putting it out through the traditional route is a tough way to make money, mostly because there's not much money in it for anyone. If a book costs $20, the actual wholesale cost to stores is closer to $10 before discounts and they can return it and get credited if it doesn't sell. (Despite this terrific arrangement, most bookstores still struggle to make a profit.)

So typically the publisher will get 45% to 50% of the list price after shipping, part of that naturally going to pay overhead: printing, design, marketing, sales, legal, and the nice New York or London offices they need to rent for all those support people. The author typically gets 10-15% of the publisher's take in the form of royalties depending on the deal and whether it's a paperback or hardback. So at 10% that means the author gets $1 per book on a $20 title, or $10,000 if 10,000 books are sold. As any author will tell you, it's not easy selling 10,000 books net—after returns are processed.

But hold on. Did you get an advance against royalties? If so, your sales have to recoup that amount first before you see another dime. If your advance was $10,000 then congratulations, you just broke even. If you sell another 400 copies net next quarter you'll rake in a big $400. That "net" number is after returns, press review copies, bookstore review copies, and all kinds of nefarious "free goods" deals that trade books for advertising or in-store positioning.

If the publisher has high hopes for your book idea and you get a fat advance of, say, $50,000 in order to enable you to go live among the natives in Papua New Guinea to write your hilarious memoir, and it's a hardback, you may need to sell "only" 30,000 or so to earn back your advance. Some manage this. But not many. In travel especially, it's not uncommon to get an advance that's $5,000 or less and never see a check after that.

Royalty rates are significantly higher with the self-publishing method known as print-on-demand (P.O.D.) books, which is attractive if you already have a following or are good at marketing. I put *The World's Cheapest Destinations* out this way and it has sold quite well through three editions. Authors do most of the heavy lifting anyway in terms of marketing and promotion—most publishers do little more than package and distribute these days—so it's only fair that you take a higher cut if you can get it.

There are disadvantages to this approach, however. No bookstore distribution, for a start, which means you better have something that will sell well online rather than to bookstore browsers. Some reviewers have a bias against any kind of self-published books since there are fewer barriers to entry and a lot of really crappy books that come through some P.O.D. publishers like iUniverse. Last, there's no advance and you'll have to lay out some of your own money up front for cover design, set-up fees, and review copies.

Self-publishing is nothing new and some authors have had plenty of success saying, "Screw you guys" and doing it themselves. Jack Canfield and Mark Victor Hansen collected 144 rejection letters from publishers for their first *Chicken Soup for the Soul* book. We know how that turned out. Some authors have started with one self-published book and have built up a whole publishing company. Print on demand just makes the process more efficient: no stacks of books in your basement that you have to peddle and ship. Some authors are going straight to Kindle and not even worrying about print. One novelist profiled in a 2010 *Wall Street Journal* story had gotten tired of publishing house rejections and uploaded her novel to Amazon's Kindle store. She eventually sold 36,000 copies, making much more on each one than she would have if she'd gotten a book deal. Take that Harper-Collins!

There's still a stigma with this approach though, even among authors. Bruce Northam says, "Just as someone in a court is considered a fool to defend themselves, publishing a book without help from a professional editor is journalistic suicide." My bank account says otherwise and I have gotten more ongoing publicity than 99% of the big publishing house's authors, but there are publications where I know I'll never get reviewed no matter what. Be aware that you'll face negativity from people who will automatically assume your book is sub-par if it doesn't have a NYC or London imprint on the inside.

A big plus though with the legit P.O.D.. publishers is that you own your book. You can sell foreign rights, get picked up by a major publisher, and sell e-book or audio book rights if demand warrants it. The publisher I use (Booklocker) sells a load of straight PDF e-books too that can be read on most any device—even ones from Apple. They'll get you into Apple's official bookstore for $75. They send me a nice monthly royalty check like clockwork and I sold the Italian rights to the second edition for a few grand in additional earnings. (Plus now I have an Italian book with my name on the spine—cool!)

This book you are holding in your hand went through this P.O.D. process because I thought putting a 2.0 book out through a 1.0 system made no sense. So I get five bucks when you buy it instead of a dollar or less and the publisher makes its fair cut as well. You probably didn't find it in a bookstore, but that matters less and less each month it seems. I buy magazines and coffee in bookstores, but I can't remember the last time I actually bought a book in one—even though I buy a lot of books. A shame, but the prices and selection in bookstores bum me out after shopping so long online. Even the superstores seem to have lousy travel sections when you're used to having everything in print (and then some) at a click of the mouse, at better prices too.

A book is a major undertaking that can consume your life for a while. Understand that writing and organizing 50,000 words or more and keeping it all interesting is exponentially harder than writing an article or even 20 articles. You had better have a lot to say on the subject and be able to say it in a way that keeps the reader's interest for a very long time. I'd bet that anyone who has asked, "How hard can it be?" and plunged in before they were ready has had a rude awakening down the line.

The first questions to ask yourself before writing even one word are, "Who is going to buy it? What's the potential market?" As Angela Hoy at Booklocker says, "It is imperative that authors have a specific market in mind before they begin to even outline their book. Most authors now seem to come up with a book idea, write the book, and then try to figure out the market they're going to sell to. Having a firm market in mind first, before the writing process, will make the book far more marketable in the end."

Any traditional publisher or literary agent will tell you the same thing. If they read anything in your book proposal after the idea pitch it will be the marketing section. They want to know who would buy this book and why. Get the idea right first, then the marketing plan. The best-written book in the world makes no money if these elements aren't in place first.

## Selling E-books Direct

E-books are not really new, so I've kept them in this old media section. They're still just electronic versions of what we're used to in printed form. They've been out in some form since we could first read text on a computer. What has changed is that the market for them is expanding exponentially and they have become easier to market. Their high growth is coming from a very low base—more than 95% of books sold are still in physical form—but there's no doubt the electronic versions will become more popular each year. The devices to read them are getting better, the prices of a Kindle, Nook, or Sony Reader have dropped to a range more people are willing to meet, and devices like the iPad are giving the curious a reason to experiment with e-books for the first time.

Right now you can buy electronic books in a multitude of formats for a multitude of devices, from plain Adobe PDF files you can read on most computers and smart phones to proprietary formats that work on one device only and can't be shared. The thing is, an author can now bypass the whole publishing establishment and get their book on all these formats relatively easily.

I sell a lot of e-books, but they are just electronic versions of my print books, either direct off the publisher's site with a link from my blog or through Amazon's Kindle store, so the marketing is the same. I split the profits with either my publisher or Amazon depending on the format. Either way the earnings are several times what I would make from a traditional publishing house---with not much more work.

Some bloggers have had some success selling e-books only, never even bothering with paper. There are big advantages to this if you have a big enough following: no distribution, no printing, and very high royalties—100% even if you're selling PDFs direct and not through others. Royalties generally start at 45% and climb from there. For example, if you go direct, Amazon pays 70%, Apple pays 70%, and Barnes & Noble pays "up to 85%" for the Nook.

The usual way this works is that someone who is known as an expert on something puts out a book of "insider knowledge" or something that compiles their other scattered writings into one central and easy-to-read document. The e-book could be on scoring frequent flyer miles, living in Costa Rica, traveling on a shoestring, or many other topics. Ironically, the ones that seem to have the most success are "how to make money on the internet" kinds of books that advise you to, among other things, write an e-book. And around it goes.

Two of the people I know personally doing the best with this on the travel side are Stuart MacDonald of Travelfish.org and Matt Kepnes of NomadicMatt.com. Stuart's are jam-packed guides to very specific destinations, while Matt's are about traveling well for less and making money online while on the move. Here's what Matt had to say in an interview on the Free Pursuits blog: "E-books can do very well or fail miserably. To make an E-book do well, you have to write about something you are an expert in. People read you for a reason so your book should complement the topics of your blog or your lifestyle. Moreover, you need to market it relentlessly. If you don't it will fail."

Stuart is in the midst of transforming his offerings, however, phasing out the PDF guides and going to a less comprehensive iPhone apps format. Time will tell if the iPhone/iPad/Touch penetration is far enough along to support this, but it's easy to envision a future where publishers and authors are making as much from downloads to smart phones as they are making now from e-books. With upheaval comes opportunity.

I am more encouraged about this area than any other though, because e-books offer a chance to move old media to new without losing much in the process and actually making life better for the creators. True, reading a book on a Kindle or iPad is still a second-rate experience compared to reading it in its physical form, but it's close enough. It's certainly a far better transition than going from a magazine to a web page—the information is still digested in a form that your brain can process easily for hours on end.

# Corporate Writing

As I was finishing up this book I dissected one issue of *Condé Nast Traveler* page by page and discovered an amazing breakdown. Out of the 240 total pages, 116 of them were actual editorial pages (including a fashion spread with almost no text). But 55 pages had "special advertising section" at the top: they were paid advertisements meant to look like articles. This means that for approximately every two pages of real editorial, including pages with just a one-sentence caption, there was one page of copy written by someone hired by an advertiser rather than by Condé Nast Publishing. Somebody got hired on the outside to write all that material, project by project. Based on what I've heard from many writers, those ad copy page jobs probably paid better too.

That's just one type of corporate writing. I'm using that phrase as a catch-all here for anything meeting a company's needs and paid for directly: website copy, brochures, sales pitches, direct mail copy, corporate blog posts, or press releases. There is also a whole big sub-industry called "custom publishing," which comprises magazines and newsletters put out by a corporation. You probably get some of them in your mailbox from the likes of Sony, GEICO, or your bank, whether you ask for them or not. Some of these magazines can be pitched like ones on the newsstand; others require getting to the right person and applying. Once you're in, you'll usually get regular work from them on an ongoing basis.

This is generally not glamorous work and it comes with its own batch of headaches and ethical issues, but it pays well. It's also a whole lot easier to get paid on time by your state tourism board, a hotel chain, or a custom publishing company with sound finances than it is to get paid by a consumer magazine teetering on the edge of bankruptcy. No nagging required.

It's hard to systematically go about finding this kind of work though; often the work finds you. The person with the need starts asking around and your name comes up. I once got an assignment on the spot at one of my wife's work parties where the hiring guy was the spouse of my wife's co-worker. Some writers get work by being available when the regular person is on vacation or sick. For these jobs networking matters—a lot.

Besides happenstance, writers often get into this kind of work by either cold calling companies, by posting their credentials and bidding on eLance or Sologig, by keeping an eye on Craigslist, or by watching sites where writing jobs are posted regularly. (See the Resources section.)

These corporate writing assignments need to come with a budget, so be prepared to state your fee right off the bat. I prefer an hourly fee if it's something with an uncertain time frame, but the person doing the hiring may need a total project number. In that case you have to do your best to estimate how much time it will take, pad it a little to be safe, and put that into a proposal.

Be willing to negotiate, but don't give away your services for cheap unless you're really desperate. If it's a reputable organization, you can bet they're paying market rates for tech support, printing, janitorial services, landscaping, payroll, and every other contracted service. So charge the market rate for the service and your experience. My rate is $40 to $50 an hour plus travel expenses depending on the job. I've seen others charge as little as $15 an hour and others charge as much as $100 an hour if they were a clear expert in a given area.

If you're good at ghostwriting books for celebrities or CEOs, you can charge even more after you've got a track record. I've billed my regular hourly rate for the six business books I've worked on as a ghostwriter, but if I signed on with someone famous getting a $200,000 advance, I'd certainly bargain for more.

Corporate writing may be a one-off gig now and then, or it may become your main source of income if you get in with a company that needs a lot of output on a regular basis. It's a hard thing to predict and plan for, but definitely worth pursuing once you have some experience and contacts. Much of it can be done from behind a desk, which may not be your initial goal in "travel writing," but that does keep your expenses low. In other cases a company may pay your expenses to have you report from a conference or convention.

# Digital Opportunities for a Travel Writer

*My skill set is a combination of web programming, travel writing, and a deep-seated desire to stay away from a cubicle!*
– Stuart MacDonald, Publisher, TravelFish.org (based in Bali)

I like the idea behind the Indian god Shiva. Besides the legend he supposedly lives atop a mountain smoking hash, he is interesting because he is the god of both destruction and creation. He can be a mean bastard when things need to be blown up and destroyed, but then he can create something better in its place.

Many cultures have deified this idea that you can't have creation without some kind of destruction and we see it in the real world when a hurricane or tornado leads to a rebuilt city with better infrastructure and safer building codes. In order for a company to reinvent itself, it often has to scale back or destroy the product that has been its main cash cow—a very painful transition. Many just can't do it and they just stop growing or they go bankrupt.

We are clearly in a transition phase right now with media and there are two sides to that story. On one hand the destruction side, where the print and network broadcast world we've known for more than half a century is crumbling down around us. Jobs disappearing, magazines folding, TV networks

> *Three years from now I will have lessened my work in print media and gravitated more to online endeavors including my own website, blog and internet magazine. My income may drop some at first (print media appears to be weakening anyway), but I expect it to level out.*
>
> – John Lamkin
> freelance writer and
> photographer

struggling, and newspapers getting thinner and thinner. That is making many travel writers scared, depressed, or sleepless. It's driving others to quit the business altogether because it's gotten too difficult.

Some see a threat in this transition, others see a huge opportunity. While the old ways are working less and less, others are finding tremendous success following a new path. Of the 52 travel writers I surveyed for this book, 28 said they were making more money now than they were making three years ago—this during the peak of a recession. I find that incredibly encouraging.

My experience is only anecdotal, but I know more travel writers making a consistently comfortable living from digital media than I ever knew making a consistently comfortable living from print writing. These people are also more confident, more relaxed, and more optimistic about the future. Let's take a look at how to get there.

# Blogging for Yourself

"Start a blog and write what you want."

That advice has turned many a head and pulled in many subscribers for "how to make money on the internet" types. And why not? It's as enticing as fat-free frozen yogurt or the promise of speed-reading. No query letters, no editors to please, no editorial calendar to fit into, and no style restraints that will hold you back. What freedom!

Remember that the root word of freedom is "free" though. That's what you'll be working for day after day, week after week, for six months to a year until your shiny new blog gets some traction—if it ever does. Instead of putting together articles for a set fee, you are putting together articles that will hopefully "be monetized" someday through advertising or other means. Your pain, your gain—if it works. Unless you have good traffic and a following, however, those ad earnings will be next to nothing. (See the next chapter for where that ad money comes from.)

For many, that's okay. They are blogging to promote themselves or their expertise, not as a moneymaker. It's their mouthpiece to sell consulting, sell books, or get noticed by the media. If you're doing this as an income generator though, be prepared for a long slog.

Like many bloggers in the early days, I started the Cheapest Destinations Blog without even thinking about whether it could ever make money. I just set it up to promote my book and to give journalists a taste of what I had to say. It was purely a promotional vehicle and a place for me to float out ideas for articles. Then Google Adsense and easy affiliate ad programs came along and I stuck some ad code on my blog. Just like that, from then on when I sat in a Wi-Fi bar and wrote a blog entry, I could rationalize that the blog was paying my bar tab. Sweet! Eventually it started making enough to pay my mortgage and I was shocked. Who knew? But this "instant success" was years in the making: the blog already had a big following by the time I started monetizing it.

Some very popular blogs today are still ad-free, however, including the very popular one from marketing godhead Seth Godin that I referenced earlier. He and other people who make most of their money from speaking or from a company they own don't really need to care if their blog makes money. It's a means to an end, a talking billboard, or a place to form the thoughts that will later go into more lucrative works. It's important to remember that stance when grousing about people who write for free. For a lot of very successful people, writing is not something you do to make money: it's something you do to communicate with your potential customers and followers. Writing is not a vocation for them, it's just a conversation, or a regular speech through typing.

It is clear, however, that the right person can turn a blog into a real job and a platform, leading to success on their own terms. I say "the right person" though because it takes a certain skill set (which can be learned) and a certain mindset (which cannot). If you run your own blog, you own it. That means the technical side, the advertising side, the administrative side, and yes, the content.

So if you're the type that likes to get marching orders and then complete the task as outlined, this is not a good path for you. If you get flabbergasted when a software program doesn't do exactly what you want it to do and you call your brother, sister, spouse, or best friend to fix it for you instead of figuring it out or reading the help screens, this is probably not your ideal medium.

WordPress upgrades can be a complete pain in the ass and I've spent untold hours rebuilding various blogs after upgrades have failed. (Now I usually pay someone else to do it.) One slash mark in the wrong place can screw up your whole design and leave you frantically combing every line of code to find the one tag that wasn't closed properly. Throwing up a blog and writing is easy. Maintaining it and making a living from it are hard.

Still, many bloggers consider this a more secure path for making *some* money at least and not being so dependent on print editors. Nobody took blogs seriously at first, but now the income potential is clearer for those that succeed at it. Like many successful print writers, David Farley says, "If I were starting out today I'd have a blog or write for blogs and websites more."

There is plenty of advice out there on getting you on the path to income in months instead of it taking you years of trial and error. Here's the main problem with trying to make money as a blogger though: ten bazillion other people are trying to make money as a blogger. If you believe some of the stats you read, there are almost as many blogs as there are readers. So once again we get into the same Darwinian struggle that exists in writing for magazines or getting a book deal: for every person making a living with their blog, there are probably at least a hundred just middling along, hoping to generate the equivalent of minimum wage for their efforts. And it's hard work on top.

I can just imagine what you may be thinking. "Hey, I bought this book for answers, Mr. Buzzkill, not a dozen reasons why I can't be a rich blogmaster of the universe! Give me the magic formula!"

If you want a shortcut, here it is: go read every post on ProBlogger and CopyBlogger and follow their links to more great advice. Heck, throw in RobbSutton.com and ThinkTraffic.com too just to be safe. It'll take a few days of bleary-eyed, non-stop reading,

But after all that you'll know close to everything there is to know about making money from a blog, including the fact that "there's no magic formula." Sorry.

So following are the initial steps. Take them and understand it's the start of a journey, not a weekend building project.

## Where's your sweet spot?

The crucial first step is to ask yourself a serious question: What can I cover better than anyone else out there?

I can't emphasize enough how important this is. If it takes you days of contemplation or the time it takes to walk the whole Appalachian Trail to figure this out, it'll be time well spent. There are a ridiculous number of generalist travel blogs out there that are pretty much interchangeable. "Here's where I went last week. Here are a few pretty photos. Here's what I did there." Yawwwwnnn.

If that's the best you can do, don't even start. That path has been walked, forged, paved, and pitted with potholes. Unless you started down that path six or eight years ago, you're too late. The same goes for a whole slew of barely-more-differentiated general categories such as family travel, city travel, and business air travel. There are people out there who already own those categories and are doing a very good job at it week after week. They are guests on CNN. They get quoted in *USA Today*. They have thousands of RSS subscribers. They come up #1 in Google for a dozen keyword phrases like, oh, "business travel blog." So unless you have a suicidal streak, don't go there.

> *I started my own website, deliciousbaby.com to write about our own family adventures, our top travel tips, and favorite products for family travel. Over time my audience grew and now I often receive offers for freelance writing because of the blog's high profile.*
>
> – Debbie Dubrow

Debbie Dubrow has been around a while and she has done a great job of promoting herself and her work. Unless you are superwoman, you will not be able to duplicate her success doing the same thing she's already doing. Did you know there's a whole convention for mommy bloggers? Or that there's one for travel bloggers? That gives you some inkling of how crowded the field is.

So think differently. Or at least think smaller. Leigh M. Caldwell is a family travel writer, blogger and broadcast personality who runs ThemeParkMom.com—a blog that's just on family theme parks. Rick Ingersoll's Frugal Travel Guy blog is about how to score frequent flyer miles without flying. Others have staked out a claim as the go-to people on specific locations, be that El Salvador, Brazil, or some second-tier city in Italy.

I've now started four blogs and in each case I filled a hole that nobody else was filling. I do mean *nobody*—I did my homework. By the time anyone else could have figured out what I was up to, I had too much of a head start for them to ever catch me. All four are profitable (even though I pay six other contributors every month) and that's not because I'm so brilliant at marketing. It's because I saw a market need and filled it. There may be fewer of those holes to fill each passing year, but other new ones pop up—partly because of new tech developments. They are there if you look around with a creative eye.

If you really keep coming up empty on your brainstorming, hire me for a short consulting session. I see a dozen holes every week in my research for articles. If I could clone myself I'd start blogs on them myself. I can sit down with you any day and find a dozen categories that come up close to empty in the search engines, with little in-depth content anywhere. As I write this it could be Android travel apps, skiing in South America, hut-to-hut hiking in the Alps, adventure travel spas that regular guys would like, or cheap hotels in Argentina. By the time you read this those may be filled by someone with initiative, but there will be plenty of others. The point is, you have the power to fill these holes yourself without waiting for permission. It's not a matter of applying for a job and hoping someone else will hire you. Put on your Nikes and just do it.

Unless you live in London, New York, San Francisco, or the Pacific Northwest (hotbeds of travel writers), there's probably nobody doing a really good job of blogging about what's worth seeing and doing in your town, or maybe even your state. Pretend you're a tourist who has never been to your area. Can you find really good, authoritative information just by doing Google searches? Try it. You may be aghast at how bad your potential competition really is, especially compared to what you can find in a $15 guidebook.

Unless you like to be Sisyphus, forever pushing a ball up a steep hill, you should find a niche that nobody else is covering and own it. Otherwise you are relying on your network, your personality, and sheer force of will to make things happen. It can still be done this way, especially if you're the popular girl everyone wants to hang out with, but you'll probably be more successful following the path of less resistance, one that you can dominate in the search engines.

Most of the 100 most popular blogs are written by a group—ones like Jaunted, Gridskipper, Gadling, HotelChatter, GoBackpacking, Brave New Traveler, Mommy Poppins, and the big portals like Uptake.com. This makes sense because they can throw up more content day after day and snag lots of search traffic. It's easy to dominate by sheer volume.

But things get interesting when you look at some of the most popular travel blogs written by just one person. Here are the top 10 independent, one-person travel blogs as of mid-2010 by Alexa rank.

**Everything-everywhere.com** - Gary Arndt set off traveling around the world in 2007 and hasn't stopped.

**DannyChoo.com** – "Danny Choo resides in Tokyo and writes about life in Japan and Japanese pop culture which includes anime, figurines, dolls, games and everything else that comes under the genre."

**NomadicMatt.com** – Matt Kepnes' site is more than a blog, but he has been chronicling his travels since 2005 and providing advice and resources on international budget travel.

**HoboTraveler.com** - Established a decade ago, a blog and resource site from perpetual traveler Andy Graham

**Elliott.org** – Christopher Elliott is a consumer travel advocate looking out for your travelers' rights and helping you avoid the many travel pitfalls and gotcha fees the industry throws out.

**FluentIn3Months.com** – Benny Lewis' guide to learning multiple languages while on the move.

**Cheapest Destinations Blog** - my guide to bargain travel around the world (travel.booklocker.com)

**PeterGreenberg.com** – the TV personality, radio show host, and author writes about avoiding travel hassles and rip-offs

**AlmostFearless.com** – "Work wirelessly. Travel the world. Do anything." Christine Gilbert's guide to traveling and having a location-independent lifestyle.

**UpgradeTravelBetter.com** – Mark Ashley's guide to "Living the first class life...at coach prices."

That's a pretty diverse lot. There's not a whole lot of commonality there except that I'm the only bozo without a domain name that matches my blog name. (Long story short, my publisher talked me into starting it many years ago and they still host it. I don't want to move it to a new domain and kill the good thing we've got going.) Plus maybe more blog readers are value-seekers than luxury-seekers.

There are many other popular one-person blogs that are probably just as popular or more so than the above, but are part of a corporate site that bundles everyone together, like Arthur Frommer's blog (at

Frommers.com), the Frugal Traveler blog at NYTimes.com, or Tim Winship's frequent flyer blog (at SmarterTravel.com). Some travel resource sites also have a blog (like the one at JohnnyJet.com), but it's just part of the mix, not the main entry door. A whole slew of others are more about lifestyle design than travel, such as the blog from *4-Hour Workweek* author Timothy Ferriss. He writes about travel now and then, but it's not the main focus.

I put that list up just to show who is getting loads of traffic and to encourage you to find a different subject matter than what they are already covering. Note also that some of them are pretty general, but that generality is backed up by a person who has become a brand name. They're big enough to attract and keep readers now no matter what they do, so they can widen the scope.

Blogging can be a rewarding path, but take the time to think through these following key questions before you launch. Once you can answer all of them clearly and with vision, you're definitely onto something.

1) What can I cover better or more thoroughly than anyone else?
2) What niche am I passionate enough about that I can write hundreds of different short articles about it for years on end?
3) What can I write about for 6-12 months that won't require going into the hole financially?
4) Do I want to be known as the expert on this subject or destination? Can I credibly become a media resource?
5) Am I willing to stick with this subject or slant for years on end in order to enjoy the payoff? Or am I willing to hire and pay other writers once it gets going?
6) Can I explain what my blog is about in an "elevator pitch" of a few sentences?
7) Could this subject area lead to other revenue sources in terms of articles, books, speaking engagements, or tours?
8) Is it something that would eventually generate advertising interest and text ad click-through from readers?

Many people have given the following advice before and I think it's the equivalent of Star Trek's prime directive: "Write about something you are passionate about." What can you stay interested in forever? Commercial considerations matter a lot and you need to find a way to differentiate yourself. But if you pick a subject or destination just for those reasons, it won't last and you will waste a lot of time and effort. Find the balance between passion and professionalism and you'll be in the sweet spot. Persist in that sweet spot and you will profit.

This self-blogging path is not for everyone though. Almost everyone I know has had their blog come crashing down at some point. (You haven't seen real panic until you see a blogger who can't log on to their dashboard or pull up their site on the web!) You've got to learn basic HTML commands, how to use plug-ins, how to edit a template, and how to edit photos and maybe even video. You have to be at least somewhat promotional and be willing to learn the basics of search engine optimization.

I also can't emphasize enough that blogging is a real commitment. Maybe not quite at the level of having a kid, but definitely up there with owning a dog. Some weeks it feels like all I did was write blog posts. Sure, you can pop out some posts in a half hour, but the good ones often take far longer when you factor in the time spent on photo editing, link insertions, SEO tweaks, tags, and formatting. There's no way around it: making money from a blog takes real work.

## From idea to implementation

If you want to forge ahead, here's how do you get started.

You can get set up quickly on an existing service like Blogger or WordPress for free, but I would strongly recommend installing WordPress or another software on your own hosting service with your own domain. If you don't, you may find you need to do so later to get to the next level and then it's a real pain and a loss of traffic while you relocate. Better to be on your own domain to start with so you will establish the brand. The domain provider and hosting service don't matter much as they're all reasonably priced now ($10 or less per month), so pick the one offering the service and interface you're most comfortable with. I've used a bunch and find it hard to recommend one as being far superior to the others. See the resources section for a few ideas.

WordPress and Blogger are both free. Typepad requires a monthly fee, but some users like it and are willing to pay. Follow the blog software instructions carefully for the install or hire someone else to do it for you. Once you're installed, the posting is simple after that. Figure out how often you want to post and go at it. Assume few people will be reading in the beginning, but act like a thousand people are because those posts will be indexed by the search engines later. I say "later" because there's this thing called the Google Sandbox which puts you on hold until the company determines you are for real. It takes time to crawl out of there and start walking, no matter how good your content may be.

Remember that the actual set-up and writing is only the beginning. Consider this wise quote from Corbett Barr, who runs the Free Pursuits and Think Traffic blogs: "If content is king, promotion is prime minister."

The greatest content in the world won't break through the clutter if you do nothing to promote it. Shy wallflowers are not successful bloggers. You will need to network, to promote, to get inbound links, to get media attention. When it's your own show, it's all on your shoulders. I'll discuss that more in the self-promotion section.

I have one last bit of advice: at first make your blog as clean and clutter-free as possible. Pick a template that will accommodate ads later, but use them very sparingly at first. You won't make much money the first six months from them anyway, so don't clutter up your site with visual distractions and code that slows down the load time. Concentrate first on saying something worthwhile and building up an audience.

# Blogging for Others

If starting your own blog from scratch and writing for free for half a year at least sounds too scary, you may want to start out writing for others. Or do both. For all the time I've had my own blogs, I've continued to write for several others as well as a freelancer.

The main advantage of writing for someone else's blog is that they will often get far more traffic than you can generate yourself. There is definite strength in numbers: multiple people are doing promotion, there is more content for the search engines to index, and there is usually someone else (not you!) taking care of the back end tweaks and upgrades. Somebody else is worrying about the revenue side. You just do your thing and get paid—a little anyway. You can concentrate on your passion without doing all the extraneous work not related to writing.

Very few blogs that hire writers pay a whole lot though, with $5 to $20 per post being where most of them seem to fall. If you spend an hour on crafting each blog post that's pretty lousy money. If you spend a half hour, you're at least above minimum wage. If you're quick and earn $30 a post, it starts to look like something that will really pay some bills. It's great experience though no matter what, and experience makes you a better writer. It makes you good at self-editing too, which is a valuable skill that editors love.

Some blogs will only require a post a week or so, but the requirements below, from a real ad on Craigslist, are more common.

*Small publisher with two part-time, freelance writing opportunities to produce 6 to 8 blog entries, or 2 to 4 web articles, per week.*

*Writers should have online experience and be comfortable writing for affluent readers, ideally with professional background in some aspect of leisure travel. Must be able to create intelligent, well crafted pieces. must be adept at online research and produce original work.*

*Work independently from your home; your hours. We retain all rights to the content you produce. Ideal second job for extra income. Experienced only; no beginners or interns. Anticipated duration: 3 months, with a possibility of extending.*
*Please reply with your contact information and attach or link to a few relevant writing samples. All replies kept confidential.*
*\* Compensation: $90-$200 per week depending on experience and volume*

See a few red flags in that ad? They say "experienced only" but are not paying you very much. On top of that they retain all rights to what you produce, meaning you can't use any of those sentences ever again in your own work. That's not necessarily a deal breaker and I've accepted that arrangement in cases where I knew I couldn't reuse it elsewhere anyway. They didn't get my best work, of course, but they didn't pay for my best work either. Everybody (sorta) wins. But take that deal with trepidation.

Figure out how much total time is involved in any blog or webzine job before deciding whether it is worthwhile for your particular situation. I have a rather dim opinion of internet writing sweatshops and content mills such as Demand Studios, Examiner.com, and Suite 101. So do most other editors and full-time professional writers. So I would only advise taking a job with one of those companies—especially Demand—if you really have no better option and you need the practice. You get paid peanuts for throwing up content designed just to attract search engine traffic rather than real readers. Most of the content is written quickly and carelessly because of the low pay and it shows. Your work usually looks horrible on the page as well, jammed with as many as six blocks of Google ads and maybe some low-CPM network ads for teeth whitening and dubious diets. (Half the revenue probably comes from readers clicking on something by mistake in the busy design.)

There are some writers on those platforms who are happy with the arrangement, but for every one of those you'll find many ex-writers who say, "Never again!" Before you sign up with any of them, carefully read the terms and conditions of what you are getting yourself into and ask to speak to others about how much they are really making each month and how many hours they are working for that amount. If it's less than a burger flipper at McDonald's—which it usually is for a year or so—it might be better to move on. With patience and a long view, however, it can be  a good match eventually. One writer I know and trust thinks Suite 101 is a cut above—if you have the right expectations.

> *I've written weekly articles at Suite101 since 2006, and I've seen a lot of writers come in all excited and gung-ho, then quit after 4 months. We're used to writing for instant cash, and it's just a different set-up at Suite. My first month there, I made all of $8, but now each month my payment gets incrementally bigger. I'm now earning about $750 a month there writing one luxury travel column each week. There are flat months too of course, and usually a dip in August. But I will not quit Suite because that is pretty dependable money.*
>
> *I hate how ad-jammed it is, but I'm proud to work at Suite, writing 400 words a week about some hotel or destination is easy as pie, and the haters have their points, but no one is making them write there. It's easy if you know how to string words together in a coherent way for the web.*
>
> – Jennifer Miner, freelance writer

There is another set of content mills that are a bit higher up on the food chain, like the ones that fall under the About.com umbrella, the sprawling AOL universe, and Uptake.com. These pay bonuses based on traffic, but they have a higher editorial standard and publish articles more meant for humans than for search engines.

I've written for multi-writer blogs about hotels, first for HotelChatter.com (now owned by the Condé Nast empire) and the

Uptake Lodging Blog. Neither has fattened my bank account much, but the posting keeps my skills and knowledge sharp when it comes to hotels and gives me an additional outlet for placing reviews of places where I'm staying when out on other assignments.

I've also written for a tour company's blog and gotten paid as much as I would for a real article, for longer and better posts. The pay for others' blogs is all over the map, but most group blog sites $25 per post or less, with some paying bonuses for traffic or revenue targets on top.

For this kind of money, you don't want to take just any blogging job. Find a good match. The idea is to put yourself in a position that is good for your profile, your niche, or the area where you want more practice writing about a subject. The money is never going to come anywhere close to meeting your monthly living expenses—unless you live in Guatemala.

The ideal situation is where you are willing to put in a lot of time and effort and in return you get a decent flat fee. A revenue share or traffic bonus is nice, but understand that it's a long time coming on those after your article starts getting search engine hits. As Miner notes above though, over time that can add up to real money—though maybe not as much as if you ran your own blog and promoted it well. Here's a similar offer from a reputable company with a good track record, BootsnAll. This was posted on LinkedIn in early 2010.

*BootsnAll is looking for passionate travel experts for new BootsnAll Travel Writer platform — a partnership with passionate travel writers to create expert-driven content on your favorite destinations and topics.*

*Current Opportunities:*
*• Destinations: Amsterdam, Australia, France, Hawaii, Indonesia, Ireland, Las Vegas, London, Mexico, South Africa, or you tell us!*
*• Themes: Adventure Travel, Business Travel, Round the World Travel, TEFL, Travel Gear or you tell us!*

***How It Works:***

• *You get to focus on your passion — travel writing; BootsnAll covers the technical aspects.*

• *Weekly tasks: feature article writing, blog posts and social media interaction*

• *Time commitment: up to 10 hours/week*

• *Compensation: base pay of $100-500/month with profit sharing of 30-40%. The base pay is based on how much content is produced. Some destinations will require more content than others....that's why the variance in base compensation.*

• *The "fine print": Just like a guide book, your content will have a copyright and non-compete, but unlike traditional guide books, BootsnAll shares the profit (up to 40%) with each writer!*

• *If you love independent travel, fancy yourself to be an expert, and want to get paid to write about a destination you love, fill out the BootsnAll Travel Writer Platform application.*

The main problem with these group blogs that pay extra based on page views or Google Adsense clicks is you end up writing for the search engines instead of writing something that sets you apart. You write things that people click on, read for 15 seconds, and then click away from. That means posts with lists in the title and posts with "best" or "worst" in the title. As Stuart MacDonald of TravelFish says, "Don't get caught up in 'top ten writing' (the ten best beaches/backpacks/bars). This type of writing is asinine and totally forgettable—even if it may pay a few of your bills. Write good quality, engaging material and people will read it and you'll perhaps develop a following."

It's hard to do that when your compensation is based on page views of individual posts. If you're going to write about the best 10 bars or beaches somewhere, at least do it for your own site or for a print outlet (they're in love with lists too) so you can make some decent money from it.

Be advised too that there are a few popular blogs out there that pay absolutely nothing to most freelancers. The Huffington Post and ConsumerTraveler.com are two of the high-profile ones. Why in the world would anyone still write for them? Because the writers want the high profile, or the traffic to their own site, or the links in to their own site, or they have a business to promote. As I'll say several times throughout this book, compensation takes many forms. I personally think a travel content website that can't afford to pay writers is a website without a clear and sustainable business model—once you get past the few exceptions like TripAdvisor—but that's just my opinion. There's no rule saying people can't keep trying to make it work.

# Writing for Webzines

Sometimes it's a fuzzy line between webzines, travel content sites, and blogs, but in general for the non-blog sites you would be writing articles meant to be entertaining or resourceful over the long term and there's less pressure to crank out words to feed the daily beast. Some of these sites are narrative publications with good stories and destination features (World Hum, Perceptive Travel, GoNomad, The Literary Traveler). Others are service-oriented sites with lots of great advice on travel and overseas experiences (BootsnAll, the Matador network, Transitions Abroad, TravelFish). Others are extensions of a print magazine, with assignments made specifically for the online part, such as Budget Travel Online and Concierge.com. Still others are good content sites that are an extension of a booking service, such as EuroCheapo.com.

For the webzines trying to put out lasting content of value, the requirements are not all that different from comparable print publications, though in some ways you have to be even better—you can't rely on huge photo spreads, charts, and sidebars to grab casual browsers. As with any publication, the easiest way to blow your chances is to fire off a query without reading a good selection of what's already been published.

> *It's easy for me to say "No thank you" to writers who obviously haven't taken the time to become familiar with the types of stories we publish. Successful freelancers know their target publications. They're familiar with the kinds of stories published, the various sections, the tone. They also are clear and concise in their writing, both in their pitches and stories. They demonstrate a professionalism and a level of writing that signals that I won't have to go through too many edits. Successful freelancers also understand that edits are part of the process. They're willing to work with editors to fine-tune stories.*
>
> - Michael Yessis, co-founder and co-editor-in-chief, WorldHum.com

Be advised that there are a lot of hucksters out there running travel content sites. A LOT. After a while you start questioning the intelligence of people who start up these new projects and wonder how in the world they can find anyone anywhere to work for what amounts to a fraction of minimum wage. Here's a real ad that ran as I was putting this book together, just so you can see how ridiculous it gets.

*Looking for detail oriented, super-accurate, geographically savvy writers that are able to produce quality content in short time frames to work on an existing Vietnam Travel Guide website." The ad continues, demanding flawless grammar and command of the English language, then finally gets to the pay part. "Project details: 5 Articles each month, 1200 - 1500 words. Payment: USD 40 per month.*

That's right: 6,000 to 7,500 words of flawless prose each week for all of $40. Most people can't even *type* fast enough to make that pay off, much less write something that's not complete gibberish. I will say throughout this book that sometimes you need to work for nothing or close to it to build up experience and a portfolio, but this is not the way to do it, by being a slave to an exploitative start-up. Run away!

# Web Publishing

*To rank well, build a site so fantastic that it makes you an authority in your niche.*
- Matt Cutts, Principal Engineer at Google

As I was writing this book, *Vanity Fair* put out a list of the top-earning individuals in Hollywood, the people making the big bucks from the movie business. The amazing part of this list wasn't that Shia LeBouf makes more than Brad Pitt, or even that the guy who has played Harry Potter for a decade makes more than both combined. The interesting part to me was that all of the people in the top 5 were either producers or had "producer/director" as their title. It's the visionaries behind the scenes—the ones taking the big risks—that are making the real money, not the faces you see on the screen.

Likewise, I'll say this many times and in many ways, but the most successful travel writers I know—and virtually all of them that manage to put six digits on their tax return—don't really think of themselves as just travel writers. They run a site or a network of sites they turned into a business. Most like the sound of "travel writer" just fine, but their business cards often have titles like webmaster, president, CEO, or publisher.

People like Stuart McDonald at TravelFish, Tom Brosnahan at Turkey Travel Planner, Gregory Hubbs at Transitions Abroad, Sean Keener at BootsnAll, and John DiScala at JohnnyJet have parlayed their passion and abilities into websites—not just blogs—that have become key destinations for readers who want to get information on where they are headed or what they plan to do with their life.

Brosnahan's TurkeyTravelPlanner.com is now by far the most authoritative and most-visited Turkey tourism site on the web. He runs a site on New England travel as well and he makes a good living as a publisher. "My income will continue to come from electronic (not paper) publishing. In the future, I will publish more work on mobile devices."

To be a web publisher you had better have a very clear vision of what sets your site apart and what need it will fill. If you get it right, you could be headed to more money than you have ever earned before. If you get it all wrong, you could be the proverbial debt-laden small business owner with maxed-out credit cards. A resource site is a bigger commitment than a blog, especially on the front end, and requires more factual research. Once it is established though, it can dominate the search engine rankings and earn good money without constant daily additions. High reward, high risk.

The good news is, starting a good content website is far cheaper than it used to be, especially if you do all the writing and posting yourself. The bad news is, it's cheaper for everyone else too. So once again, you had better pick a subject, niche, or destination that you can cover better than anyone. EuropeForVisitors.com has already been done and the site has got a 10-year head start on you. Ditto for anything general about Hawaii, New York City, family travel, or cruises. When it's your own baby, you need to think like a mix between an inventor and a marketing maven. Where's the hole in the market?

Do this right and it can

> *If I were starting out now, I'd do pretty much what I've done: I'd pick a strong topic and build an "evergreen" editorial travel-planning site that would bring in traffic and revenue month after month, year after year.*
>
> – Durant Imboden, publisher, EuropeforVisitors.com

become a reliable source of income. As Edward Hasbrouck, author of *The Practical Nomad* says, "For the last two years I've made more from my website than from book royalties. I think the biggest key to my success has been a focus on building my personal brand equity rather than on 'selling my writing.'"

# Digital Corporate Writing

I know one travel writer and blogger whose day job involves a very different kind of writing: she's a ghost blogger. Getting a nice paycheck instead of byline glory, she takes business leaders' ideas and puts them into a form that works online. The business leader gets his or her thoughts out on a regular basis online, but writes a check instead of spending hours toiling away at it.

There's also plenty of corporate travel writing going on. Someone has to fill up hundreds of pages of content on all those official tourism bureau websites and more often than not there's nobody on staff with the time and talent to get it done. So the tourism bureau farms out the writing work to a freelancer. Many hotels and attractions—if they're smart enough to realize they need good content to show up in the search engines—will also hire freelancers to beef up their pages. (Search engines like pages that have 400 or more words of text on the page, not swirling Flash sites with lots of pretty photos and no info.)

Most of these jobs are not advertised, partly because the organizations doing the hiring don't want everyone to know they can't do it in house, partly because they're rather hire someone they know already or who has been recommended. So play nice with your local tourism bureau because you never know what jobs are being discussed in meetings. Join any local writing groups that may exist in your area and network with other freelancers. Often the first question a writer gets when they turn down a project offer is, "Do you know someone else who would be good for this?"

Other times the organizations don't know they need someone until it's pointed out to them. Some writers with the right cold calling temperament have had success in pitching their services to tourism boards, independent hotels, and attractions with terrible websites. To do this, you need to clearly illustrate where the deficiencies are (outdated information, poor search engine placement, not enough content to draw visitors) and clearly show how you can remedy the situation. Be ready to discuss what you would charge—per hour or per project—and be ready to illustrate what kind of return on investment they should see in six months or a year.

Still others get steady work writing e-mail newsletters, writing a tourism board's blog, or handling a thinly staffed organization's efforts in reaching out through Twitter and Facebook. Even if the organization has a full-time public relations person, that person is probably plenty busy just writing press releases and interfacing with media on stories, interviews, and press trips. If you can ease the writing burden without costing them a fortune, many organizations will see you as an answer to their problems.

## Online Income Streams

I've alluded to the fact that most of the real success stories out there in the travel writing world are creators who own what they publish, not the hired guns writing a feature or two a month for the glossies. For the uninitiated though, the whole idea of advertising creating a sizable income seems dubious, ambiguous, maybe lacking in substance. "I wouldn't even know where to start when it comes to selling advertising," is a common refrain. That's understandable. We're trying to be writers here, not sales reps.

Anyone who has been to journalism school has had it completely and repeatedly jammed into their brain that the revenue side of publishing should be strictly separated from the editorial side. That "Chinese Wall" has always been full of holes—note the correlation between advertisements and content in your typical glossy travel magazine—but at print pubs with a staff of 100, this was relatively easy to pull off most of the time. The low-overhead web is a different story. When a successful site is a one-person operation, how do you split the commercial from the creative? Both functions fall on the same shoulders.

Fortunately, this advertising process has become so automated now that you only have to do any real selling if you're booking direct ads for your site. The rest of it can be as simple as pasting in some code and working out the payment details. That won't make you rich, but it's certainly no sweat to implement.

Here are the general buckets into which most ad revenue streams fall.

# Google Adsense

This advertising system is probably the most common and it's what is most likely to be the first thing to take blogging from a hobby to a moneymaker for most people. You install a piece of code where you want the ads to run, Google serves up text ads relevant to what is on the page, and you get paid each time someone clicks on one of the ads. Every month you pass $100 in earnings (previous balances are rolled over), you get a check or direct deposit. It's dead simple and effective, which is why Google has thrashed every other Internet company when it comes to earnings: they're getting a big piece of every click and advertisers love them because they can clearly track the results.

The earnings on your end are mostly beer money at first though and are never worth quitting your day job for until you get traffic in the hundreds of thousands of visitors and have a high click rate. If we assume you earn an average of 20 cents per click, it takes 100 reader clicks on ads just to get to $20. To make $100 you would need 500 clicks. If your click-through percentage is 1%, which is actually pretty good, then you would need 50,000 monthly page views to earn $100. If you managed to earn 60 cents per click because of your subject matter, those 50,000 page views would earn you $300. Better, but still barely enough to make a car payment. And only a few travel blogs get that many hits a month. So you probably need to have traffic in the millions to live off Google alone.

As a rule of thumb, most bloggers and webmasters make between $10 and $50 from every 10,000 page views—the high number coming from making the ads as prominent as the content or blogging about a subject that generates high keyword prices. Getting just 10,000 page views a month is a challenge though, so this alone is not going to cut it for a while.

Besides that, the ads are ugly. That's part of the reason they work so well—they blend in with the text and are matched to the content—but slapping a bunch of Google AdSense blocks up is a sure way to kill the aesthetics of your site or blog. The key is finding the right balance between the best placements for earnings and managing to avoid annoying your readers and looking cheap.

It's hard to avoid Adsense because it's the simplest and most effective ad tool to integrate, but only a few sites depend on this as their main revenue stream.

## Aggregated Affiliate Advertising

Companies such as Commission Junction, LinkShare, AffiliateFuture, and Google Affiliate Network are also a godsend for individual bloggers and publishers. In one spot you can sign up for the affiliate programs for multiple companies and you get payment for combined earnings. So if someone clicks on an Expedia ad and books a $200 hotel stay, you may make $8. If someone else buys a suitcase from eBags, maybe another $5. A few more transactions and let's say your total is $55. You haven't made a lot from any one vendor, but a couple months later Commission Junction sends you a check or makes a deposit for the combined amount—all $55. This allows you to match the ads to what you are writing about, choosing from the integrated dashboard that presents all the banners and text links from the different programs you've joined in one place. You can even link to individual products, cities, or hotels in the text of what you are writing.

The main disadvantage of this, as with all affiliate ads, is that you are doing all the work but only getting a fraction of the purchase as commission—typically 3% to 10%. If nobody purchases anything from that REI ad you had up for two months, REI just got lots of branding exposure without spending a cent. You only get paid if you deliver a paying customer. So you have to experiment and test to find out what works for your readers.

The other disadvantage is that you need to be accepted to each program within the aggregator individually. So Travelocity may approve you and Hotels.com may reject you, or vice versa. There's no explanation as to why this happens. I have sites with huge traffic that are #1 in Google for key travel phrases that still get rejected and I have no idea why. Some sites approve everyone, others are very strict. You won't know until you start applying.

Some websites have great success with affiliate programs and for others it's a complete bust. Often this depends on the subject matter. If you write about Las Vegas or Orlando, it's very easy to get bookings by integrating hotel program ads. If you write about some kind of product regularly, such as cameras, then it's easy to tie in camera model links and earn a commission from photography accessories. Not so easy is earning money from a straight travel or destination site, especially if you cover an obscure destination with no chain hotels and only one airline. A few months of experimentation will tell you whether these ads are a waste of time or a godsend.

Another reason to consider them though is the future: these are about the only ads that pay off when someone is reading your blog from a mobile device like an iPhone. Those tiny screens don't render banner ads or Google text ads very well. But if you have affiliate links in the actual blog post, as you would when reviewing a product, the text is normal size and readers are far more likely to click through and buy that book, CD, or backpack.

## Direct Affiliate Advertising

Some companies are not set up through the big clearing houses and you need to join up with them individually. This is more of a hassle to keep up with and you need to hit a higher minimum to get paid, but it can be worth the trouble for the right company.

Amazon is the most obvious case and in some ways they invented the whole idea of affiliate advertising, using it to grow rapidly in the early years and leave everyone else in the dust. When I first started out with Amazon I had trouble hitting the minimum of $25 in commission in any fewer than six months. I still earn almost nothing from their UK and Canada versions. The U.S. one rocks for me now though, partly because the more items you sell, the higher your commission goes. In some months I'll hit the 7% commission level and will earn a few hundred dollars in 30 days. They'll pay you in gift certificates at a lower minimum than cash, which I've stuck with over the years because it gives me a ready stash of gift money for birthdays, weddings, and holidays. Amazon seems to sell almost everything too, so almost anytime you mention a product you can insert your own affiliate link and potentially make a commission.

Others that run their own programs include World Nomads travel insurance, the Trip.com booking site, AirTreks round-the-world tickets agency, Asian hotel site Agora, and Booking Wiz. If a company like this is a great match and your site is ready for prime time, get in touch and apply. If you're not getting big traffic though, I'd start with Amazon and the aggregate sites. Otherwise you could be waiting a year to hit the minimum payout and get your earnings. That's frustrating.

## Network Display Advertising

Network advertising is a waste of time unless you are getting thousands of visitors a day. Otherwise the ones that will accept you are a "race to the bottom" group that will pay you somewhere around 50 cents to $1.50 per 1,000 visitors. That is known as the CPM rate and it can go to $5 or more for a really good targeted network, but that's still not all that much. Serve up 50,000 banner ads at a $5 CPM and you earn $250.

That's for a good network. Unfortunately, most of the networks are just serving clients trying to get as many eyeballs for as little money as possible. On top of this low rate, they probably won't fill 100% of your ad space. Let's say for argument's sake that they fill half. If you get 1,000 page views per day, or 30,000 in the course of a month, with a $1 CPM and 50% fill you've earned a grand total of...$15. Selling just one direct ad at $30 a month would double your earnings for that space.

This gives you some sense of why magazines and newspapers are not finding much salvation on the web. Those banner ads are no replacement for what they're running in print. Networks can make sense for filling remnant space on a popular site with big traffic, but if you're just starting out it's not worth considering.

## Paid Display Ad Listings/Sponsors

This is what most people think of when they imagine running their own site or blog. "I'm terrible at selling. How can I cold-call people and ask them to buy ads?"

In reality, you're very lucky if you can pull in any of this advertising at all for quite a while. You either need to be very specialized or have really high traffic. At that point you may be able to sell some direct ad blocks, or companies may even contact you. (So always have an "Advertise Here" page with rates or contact info just in case.) This is generally the most lucrative kind of advertising you can get since the companies are paying to reach your specific audience and you set the price.

It takes work to make it happen though. There is more sales work involved in this kind of advertising than with any of the others mentioned in this section. Nothing is automated and it's not for the timid.

If you manage to make some sales, you could get anywhere from $25 to $250 a month from a single ad on the home page. If your site is really popular, several times that amount. So get popular and the money will follow. It may even land in your lap. I don't really sell all that many ads: I respond to inquiries about advertising. There's a big difference.

## Text Links

Many bloggers and web publishers make a significant amount of their income from text links. These are links to another website, usually a commercial provider, which is paid for on a monthly basis. The companies usually hope some visitors will click on that link, but the key reason they buy these ads is for SEO purposes, to aid their search engine positioning. Google rankings are partly a popularity contest: the more inbound links you have containing specific phrases, the higher you'll probably show up in searches for those phrases. This is a way for these companies to gain more inbound links and they're willing to pay $10, $50, or $100 a month for the placement.

This is yet another reason to specialize: the companies and agencies that buy text ads want to buy them from sites that rank very high in search engines themselves. If you can dominate a niche, you'll get more of these contacts knocking at your door.

The danger in selling text ads is it's a practice Google, otherwise known as Big Brother of the Internet, isn't at all fond of. The cynical say the company doesn't like the ad competition. Google sees it as people trying to game the system. So while there's nothing illegal or (in my opinion) immoral about selling text ads, it has the potential to get you slapped on the wrist by the self-proclaimed boss of the web.

I don't know of anyone who has actually suffered real harm in actual search results by doing this, but Google does frequently knock down a site's Pagerank by a couple notches in the little toolbar some people have on their browser. Ironically, the only people who really care about the ranking on that little toolbar are...the people who buy text links!

You can do this direct yourself or you can offer space on networks that match buyers and sellers, such as TextLinkAds.com.

# Free Stuff

If you are influential in any field, companies and PR agencies will start offering you free stuff so you will publicize their brand. Movie stars have designers begging them to wear their clothes. Rock bands have musical instrument companies begging them to use their guitars and drums. Athletes not only get free clothing and equipment: they get fat checks in return for wearing and using it all.

To a less lucrative extent, this phenomenon exists in the writing world as well. The most obvious example is a hotel or visitors' bureau sponsoring a writer's trip, which leads to press coverage for everyone. People who blog about theme parks seldom pay to take the kids on a theme park vacation. Music writers don't pay for concerts. Auto writers drive a different car every two weeks without paying for anything but gas. Fashion writers have great wardrobes draped upon them by clothing companies. I can pack a whole suitcase with travel apparel people have sent me to review for Practical Travel Gear.

There's a whole ethical spectrum to all this, with some writers recoiling from the whole idea and some editors banning the practice. At the other end are people who will write gushing praise about anything landing in their lap, whether the product or service was great or not.

Most of us reside somewhere in the middle, accepting freebies when it makes sense but still writing about them with honesty. I think it is also fair to put some kind of blanket disclosure statement on your site or blog saying that you receive these trips/rooms/shoes or whatever on occasion. Some sites ask for a disclosure at the end of each post.

It seems to me that the ethical issues of this have become less of an issue as the gatekeeper press has faded in significance. If people don't trust a writer, they'll go elsewhere with one click. Most magazines don't disclose anything about advertiser influence or whether they sent back those shiny gadgets after reviewing them and frankly I couldn't care less anyway as long as the review is accurate, balanced, and well-supported. Just be advised there is potential for conflict whenever you get something for nothing. Be honest and true and you'll sleep better at night.

## Sponsored Posts

I personally feel that this income option usually goes over the slimy line, but if you have some success with your blog or website, sooner or later someone will approach you offering to pay you for mentioning their company and linking to them. Think of it as product placement for the blogging world. It's up to you whether this is kosher or not, but I have to bring it up because some bloggers and site owners use it to make some easy cash.

Once again, there's even a venture-financing-backed company bringing the buyers and sellers together in an automated fashion: Izea.com. (It used to be called PayPerPost.com, but they changed names after catching lots of flack.)

# Developing a Niche

*It is impossible to produce superior performance unless you do something different than the majority.*

- John Templeton, legendary investor and mutual fund company founder

There was a popular business book out last decade called *Blue Ocean Strategy*. The core point of it was that you can get all bloodied trying to fight in a crowded market, but if you can create a whole new market that didn't exist before, you're sailing in your own blue ocean. The successful examples of this are around you every day: Apple, Google, CarMax, Netflix, Twitter, and the Flip Ultra video camera, for a start.

It's hard to create a whole new market in this travel field, but it's not all that hard to focus on one thing and do it better than anyone instead of trying to be a generalist pen for hire. Just being a general "travel writer" puts you in a bloody pool and you'll have a hard time getting higher wages than anyone else doing the same thing.

Getting known as the expert on independent boutique hotels in Italy is a whole different story. You can count your competition on one hand. The same goes for single track biking in New England or kayaking in Belize.

Brad Olsen of CCC Publishing has written four books with *Sacred Places* in the title. He *owns* that market. Joan Petersen of Gingko Press has a whole bunch of *Eat Smart In____* books that cover Mexico, Peru, India, Sicily, Brazil, and other great food destinations. She certainly doesn't have to prove to anyone that she's an international cuisine expert.

While being a jack of all trades can make sense for some people, especially part-time writers, not having at least one specialty can be detrimental in the long run. If you write about anything or any place, you are putting yourself into a very big sea of other similar writers and the only way you can stand out is to be a far superior or more professional writer. I know a few successful feature writers who get away with this because they are so good at what they do and have such a great track record that they are able to be generalists. Whatever assignment comes their way, they can cover it well: luxury Caribbean this month, budget Bali next week, the architecture of Barcelona next. They are curious enough and observant enough—and talented enough writers—that they can make any of these stories sing. Even for them though there are some assignments they just won't take because they'd be too bored with the subject matter. They know their skills, but also the limitations of their interest.

For most of us, we need to be identified with something specific to get assignments from editors, to sell books, or to build up a following on the internet. This can be as general as European train travel or as specific as wine tourism in France on the destination side, as general as family travel with teens or as specific windsurfing on Lake Tahoe on the "how to" side. The more general the subject though, the harder it is to stand out.

As the media gets sliced and diced more ways and also gets more competitive, editors are increasingly looking for writers who have something special to offer. As Sean Keener, CEO of BootsnAll says, "Find a niche that you are passionate about. Don't follow the crowd. Define what makes you unique."

This doesn't mean that the wine tourism in France person can't write about B&Bs in Vermont or the Lake Tahoe windsurfing person can't write about Ecuador, but neither one can switch specialties every two months, continually ditching the old one for good. I can write about luxury travel just as easily as budget travel at this point in my life, but with books out about cheap travel, I have a much easier time getting noticed and quoted in the media for the latter. Editors actually call me with assignments sometimes, solely based on my visibility in this subject area. If they want an article about windsurfing, they're going to call that windsurfing specialist instead.

So what are you an expert at, or in what area could you easily become an expert? Think long and hard about this and make sure it's a subject or place that inspires passion in you. Turn off the electronics and take a hike—literally. Get out of the office and find someplace quiet to think. Take a lesson from Pixar: they didn't come up with their nine-for-nine terrific movie ideas sitting around a conference room. They always headed to a cabin 50 miles out of the city to do their most important creative thinking.

This thought process is important because the focus needs to connect. There's no sense in becoming the European river cruises expert if you don't like ship cabins or hanging out with retired people. You don't want to become the Minneapolis travel specialist if you hate the cold and want to move south as soon as possible.

Specializing is especially important in the blogosphere. Starting one today about general family travel or restaurants in Paris would be an exercise in futility unless you already have a huge following as a book author or TV show host. It's too hard to stand out from the pack. Find a niche that's not so crowded already or choose a truly unique way to cover that place/subject.

Darrin Rowse, who runs the ridiculously popular ProBlogger site, succinctly explained in one particular post why a niche is so important. I'm paraphrasing a bit here, but these are the key reasons:

1) **A niche blog attracts more readers naturally.** People come back because they care about the subject and want to learn and interact.

2) **A niche blog is easier to monetize.** Specific topics draw specific advertisers and those ads get a more favorable reaction from readers.

3) **Niche blogs do better in search engines.** If you're all over the map, Google doesn't know what your site is about. If you specialize, it's more likely to be seen as authoritative.

4) **Niche blogs build credibility and profile.** Experts draw attention from the media, from people who want to hire experts. Who has ever said, "Get me a generalist on the phone"?

Nicholas Gill has authored several guidebooks and has appeared in top-tier publications such as the *New York Times*, *National Geographic Traveler*, *Condé Nast Traveler*, and *Caribbean Travel &*

*Life*. Still, he says, "I think it is becoming more and more important to start your own website and carve out your own niche. The web allows a writer to find extremely select audiences with narrow interests from all around the world." He has followed his own advice with Newworldreview.com, a webzine about on Latin American food, drink, and travel.

Moon Handbooks author Joshua Berman has a clear niche, being known as one of the foremost authorities on traveling or living in both Nicaragua and Belize. "Have a strong web presence with a definite niche, whether that be a particular destination that you know very well, or whether it be an activity like volunteering abroad in different countries, or an expert on Spanish schools in Mexico ... develop a solid expertise/platform and people will find you.

How do you know if you're onto something? Try the old entrepreneur's trick of condensing that specialty or blog is into a short "elevator pitch." If you can summarize your specialty or your blog's slant in a couple sentences at a cocktail party, you're probably on the right track.

What would you like your future bio to say? Could you explain *that* during a short elevator ride or a cocktail party introduction? Figure out and then find a way to make it happen.

## The Part-time Expert?

It's perfectly fine to develop your niche as a part-time freelancer writer as well. Many well-known bloggers have a day job. Many guidebook writers don't depend on that pay to cover their annual expenses: they lead tours, they have a flexible office job, they work for an NGO abroad, or they do seasonal work of some kind the rest of the year.

> *I think it's rare to be able to make a full-time existence from guidebook writing. In addition to cultivating your freelance credentials, work on finding a job that's flexible enough to let you go to half-time or take extended periods off when you have a book to do. Also, if you live in a place that's a desirable destination but where there aren't that many travel writers—or at least those that can write in English—you might find it a faster way to establish your credentials. (If you try to go this route, do your research to find what the money-making destinations are.)*
>
> - Grace Fujimoto, acquisitions director at Avalon Travel (Moon Handbooks and Dog Lover's Companion series)

Most of the travel writers you see on press trips or at conferences are not full-time writers. If you attend a Society of American Travel Writers meeting, you'll find that most of the people there are of retirement age. They don't need to do this for a living. They're doing it because they enjoy it.

More power to them. They might only make $25 writing an article for GoNomad or a small weekly newspaper, but they're traveling around southern France or the Caribbean for a week on somebody else's tab, so that doesn't faze them. Telling them they shouldn't work for so cheap is going to fall on deaf ears. They're having a blast.

If this really bugs you, find another profession to pursue. It's the reality of the marketplace and it's only going to become more common as print work dries up.

If you are in a position to be a part-time travel writer, with no concerns about the financial payoff, then in a way you are the ideal candidate for a happy career as a freelancer. You can get more assignments, take more trips, and enjoy yourself more while traveling than someone who actually has to make it all pay the bills.

I don't have any hard data on this, but I'd guess the majority of travel writers going on press trips regularly are either supported by a working spouse, have another job that pays the bills, or are retired. So if you are one of the above, join the club. It's a happy club to be in.

For part-timers with no money concerns, breaking in is pretty easy. There are a zillion small print publications and websites that pay nothing or a nominal amount that may as well be nothing. Some of them, like ConsumerTraveler.com, actually have a sizable audience of 100,000 or more readers every month. You may not earn money, but you'll earn some form of glory.

On some other sites you'll toil away in obscurity, especially if you join up now with one of the content sweatshops like Examiner.com or one of the searchbait content mills like Demand Studios. These are good for writing practice and the occasional bottom-feeder press trip invite, but not much else. If you're going to crank out as much content as they usually want, you're much better off in the long run starting your own site and owning the content forever.

# Self-promotion

Mastering a niche and being an expert at something is essential now, but that still only gets you halfway to success. Like the proverbial tree falling in the forest when nobody is around, you'll still toil in obscurity if a few key things don't happen to raise your profile. Making those things happen isn't magic: success requires a concerted effort and a self-promoting mindset.

Many writers hear "self-promotion" and cringe, the same way many indie rockers and struggling painters do when they're starting out. Without some smart self-promotion, however, it's almost impossible to create any sort of income from your art. Someone who's noisier and more visible will get that income instead.

Promoting yourself doesn't mean you have to be a loudmouth jerk who dominates every conversation and bores everyone around. It doesn't mean steering every conversation subject toward yourself, online or off. It certainly doesn't mean putting up 30 tweets or Facebook status updates every day. After all, many of the most successful nonfiction writers are, by all accounts, self-effacing people who are quite pleasant to be around. (Who has ever called Rick Steves a self-absorbed jerk?) They've found a way to be visible without being aggressive about it.

There are a lot of successful bloggers out there who are terrible schmoozers at parties and lots of book authors that never brag about their accomplishments. I'm not active on Facebook and many successful writers think Twitter is the clearest evidence yet that the movie *Ideocracy* is coming true before our eyes.

Most writers who make real money at this are visible somehow though If not one of these methods, than something else instead. They have picked a few paths to recognition and are promoting themselves actively on a regular basis by doing the right things for their situation, week in and week out. They seek out opportunities instead of waiting for things to fall in their lap.

Each method outlined below is involved enough to warrant its own book or workshop, so learn more about each as you go and figure out what's best, but here are summaries of a few key visibility tactics. Some are more important to bloggers or webmasters than they are to pure freelancers, but consider each a tool that can be employed at different levels of commitment depending on your own situation.

## Your own blog

For some people this is a great vehicle. For others it's a waste of time: don't assume it's an automatic need. A blog works best for a defined niche that lends itself to lots of ongoing content and reflections on changes in the environment or marketplace. If you intend to be seen as an expert on something or someplace specific, by all means forge ahead. If you are likely to build a following by bringing new material to your tribe every week, then a blog is essential. It's a great mouthpiece, a search engine magnet, and eventually something that will get you media attention and writing assignments.

But what if you're a guidebook writer covering different areas every few months? Or a feature writer with no specific beat? Or a regular columnist or blogger for someone else who has a hard enough time coming up with ideas for that each week? In those cases, a blog is probably not a good idea. It will just suck away more time and energy without accomplishing your goals or making you more money. Many writers should be bloggers, but definitely not all of them.

Keep in mind that a blog can turn into an all-consuming endeavor that takes up more and more of your time as it grows. Diving into this commitment without clear goals and expectations is a big mistake. You may need one of these, but if you don't at this particular moment, there's no point in doing it halfway.

## Your own website

A blog can be a good promotional tool or platform, but when it comes to self-promotion for freelancers, a portfolio site is essential unless you never want to write for anyone else. This is the first thing I as an editor seek out when I'm deciding to hire someone, no matter what they've said in their query letter. It's also what I expect to see pop up on the first page of Google when I search their name. If, instead, I get their Facebook page with shout-outs to their friends, drunken party pictures, and a blog about their cat, I start questioning their status as a writer.

Even if you do have a travel-related blog, either build a portfolio site as well or make a really good "About Me" page on your blog, with links to your best work. This is as close as you'll ever get to free advertising for your services and thus the easiest return on investment decision you'll ever make, even if you spend some money on a designer. See the Resources section for a few ideas on where to get started.

## Some search engine optimization (SEO) knowledge

If you build a portfolio site or blog and then neglect to include the keywords relating to your niche, you are invisible to anyone searching for that niche. The basics of SEO are elementary: figure out how you want people to be searching for you or your site and make sure you have done the right things to get your site high up in those results. Google ranking is complicated, but it's primarily a popularity contest. You can't win that contest for "cheap flights," but with some work you can win it for "best New York sidewalk food carts," "northern England barge tours," or "spelunking in Missouri."

If you are the foremost expert on urban hiking the mountains around Los Angeles (as one blogger I know is), then obviously you need to have things like "urban hiking expert" and "Los Angeles" in your title or description and in the words of the actual text somewhere. Each separate page or blog entry needs its own set of keywords and phrases. These go in the text and they also go in something called "metatags" that are instructions to the search engine bots.

In the next phase, you want to get people to link to you or you put your own link in things you write elsewhere on the web, preferably using those key phrases that describe your expertise. Links to your name don't hurt either, especially if your name is not real unusual and you want to rise above the others with that same name. (On that note, if you do have a really common name, find a way to differentiate yourself, like adding your middle name, a nickname, or an initial.) Writers who are easy to find get assignments, get interviewed, get noticed, get book deals. Those who are not easy to find online will struggle more and more as the years go on.

There are ways to build up many of these links naturally, through message board signatures, profiles on sites where you're an active member of some kind, or blogs where you make a comment. Plus there's social media platforms...

## Social media presence

This one is a loaded hand grenade. It's an easy—maybe too easy—way to communicate with a group of others at once. Some very successful writers I know pooh-pooh this whole phenomenon and think it reflects the decline of both the written word and civilization itself. Others think Twitter is the greatest invention since the microphone. They can't wait to get up in the morning and tell everyone who will listen what they ate for breakfast and what their cute kid said on the way to school. Some have found a way to profit from this oversharing, getting thousands of visitors to their blog every day and turning that into enough income to fund their travels around the world.

> *Joining NATJA gave me the chance to learn firsthand from established professionals and an opportunity to build a personal network. I also attended a workshop given by National Geographic Traveler where I learned a lot about how things work in the print magazine world. Probably the most important key to success was becoming active in social media. I was an early adopter of Twitter but didn't really "get it" until more than a year after setting up my account. While on my own in Paris for several weeks, Facebook and Twitter became my primary means of communication with friends and family back home. When I returned, I continued to develop my following. In the time since, the majority of my new industry contacts have come through Twitter, Facebook, LinkedIn, and other social networking sites.*
>
> – Lanora Mueller, part-time travel writer

Others do nothing or close to it on these platforms and still get plenty of work writing for others.

I'm somewhere in the middle in this social media debate. Obviously I owe much of my success to blogging, but I try to write informative or entertaining posts that have lasting value instead of perishable drivel. I'm on LinkedIn and use it to track down professional contacts. I'm on Twitter, but reluctantly. I seldom spend more than five minutes a day on it because I've found anything over that has a diminishing return. Like a few other holdouts that make an actual living as a writer, I'm not active on Facebook—though I do have a fan page set up for a few websites. (Personally, if old classmates can't find me when my name generates 40 pages of results on Google, some of them with phone numbers listed, do I really want to hear from them on a personal page?)

I see the power of these platforms, but I also see the productivity killing machines they can become and the feelings of addiction they inspire in some. I've seen travel writers miss whole conversations—important ones—because they were looking down at the glow on their handheld screens, scrolling through messages from people an ocean away.

I can't tell you what will work for you, but for many people blogs are a proven moneymaker. Twitter, Facebook, LinkedIn, FourSquare, and whatever the next flavor of the year turns out to be are not. They can be good networking tools and one or more may help you build a tribe of followers or connect with a few editors or key PR people. For others, it'll just waste time they could be using to create something that people will still be reading a year from now instead. As a study quoted in Wired magazine said, "Media multitaskers are suckers for irrelevancy: We are training our brains to pay attention to the crap."

Sites like Stumbleupon, Digg, and Reddit can send a burst of traffic to your site, so some bloggers promote on these relentlessly, but that traffic is like a sugar high that quickly fades. Few of those readers return later

Use these tools as judiciously as you would any other time commitment and they can pay off if you have a plan and measurable metrics. Spend half your day on them because they distract you from real work though and it can be quite counter-productive. Remember, being busy isn't the same as getting things done.

Also remember that while Facebook, Twitter, and LinkedIn seem invincible now, so did AOL, Yahoo, and MySpace at different times. Remember when podcasts and Second Life were getting all the buzz?

Put your most important work on sites you own, not on platforms that could fade away, go into decline, or make their privacy policies so invasive that they're practically committing identity theft. People have often compared social media platforms to a giant high school, so it's important to remember what happened to those most popular kids in your own high school, 10 or 15 years down the line.

Remember, these social media platforms are a means to an end, not an end in themselves. As Jason Fried, founder of 37Signals, said in an *Inc.* interview, "It really bothers me that the definition of success has changed from profits to followers, friends, and feed count. This crap doesn't mean anything. If a restaurant served more food than anyone else but lost money on every diner, would it be successful? No."

## Physical networking

One of the best time-tested ways to raise your profile is to widen your network of friends and associates in your field. If anything, the digital world has enhanced the power of personal connections. A link from a high-profile blog can mean more than a quote in a major magazine. And all you had to do was get in touch with a friend.

Join local writing groups if that's an option and attend a conference now and then where you can meet other travel writers and editors. When people know who you are, they're more likely to read what you write, recommend what you write, and hire you or recommend you when the opportunity comes up. I'll take five contacts I've met face-to-face over 100 new Twitter followers any day. There's a stronger bond that's longer lasting.

The good news is, those social media platforms have made finding and meeting the right people easier than ever. When I'm in a new city I'll look up a writer or two and get together in person. Before the web it was really hard to track people down and meet them. Now it's done with a few clicks. No excuses anymore: get out from behind the laptop, put the crackberry away, and have discussions without distractions.

Many organizations are out there that will formalize this networking. See the resources section at the end for the web sites of the Society of American Travel Writers, North American Travel Journalists Association, American Society of Journalist and Authors, and others. As the print world some of these organizations are inextricably tied to fades in importance, the organizations themselves are less relevant. Still, for a couple hundred bucks in annual dues, they can be worth it for jump-starting your contact list and access to PR people and press trips.

Others, however, are free and are more relevant to non-print writers. Check out the MediaKitty.com community and the Travel Blog Exchange.

## Message boards

You don't hear as much about these as you did before people started sectioning themselves off in Facebook groups, but message boards are as powerful a place as ever to create a presence and build your credibility. Whether your expertise is Tuscany, barbecue joints, or skiing in Idaho, there's probably a message board somewhere with people interested in that subject. Find it, join it, become a part of it. Put a link to your site in your signature and you'll find people following that to your site. Link to an article you've written now and then (make sure it's useful) and people will click on that. If you're really an expert, over time you'll build authority and you'll learn a few things you didn't know as well.

If you ever plan to write a book, hanging out on message boards can give you a good sense of what people are curious about. Before I put out my first book, *The World's Cheapest Destinations*, I spent a lot of time reading questions from soon-departing around-the-world travelers on Lonely Planet's Thorn Tree. The questions that came up over and over again (and still do) were, "How cheap is it to travel in [insert country]" and "Will my budget of [insert amount] be enough to last six month in [insert itinerary]?" I didn't have to do any market research beyond that. I knew there was no book out there answering these questions and if I created one that was good it would keep selling year after year. After three editions and more than 12,000 copies sold net, I think I can safely say I was correct.

If you want to become an expert on some place or subject, first figure out what needs to be known. Then when you have all the answers, you're at least halfway there. Now share them.

# Following others' blogs

Similar to being active on message boards, most successful bloggers are those who are actively in touch with other bloggers. They have related blogs set up in their RSS streams, they read them, and they comment on posts that interest them. This does two things: it creates a link back to your own blog (you insert your website when you make a comment) and it gets you on the radar of that blogger and his/her readers. People with like interests gravitate to each other . Successful bloggers make a tremendous number of valuable contacts through this simple action. Many of those bloggers become readers of what you are writing and they link to your work when they see something they think is notable.

Like many of the best self-promotion methods, this is painless and free. As usual, just keep it reasonable—being annoying will have the opposite effect you intended. Spending too much time on this and not enough on content creation becomes futile past a certain point.

# Guest Posts

One sure-fire way to expand your profile and get a valuable link back to your site(s) is to write a guest post for someone else's blog. Sure this is another "writing for free" opportunity that some will frown upon, but it's a powerful tool. You want to look up and not down when pitching a guest post to a blogger: aim for a site that has far higher traffic and more followers than your own.

Drawing from your expertise, craft a short article that's a great fit for that blog's readers—preferably in plain text or HTML to make it easy on the host. A guest post is often welcome because it saves the host a day of filling the blog with her own material and it provides an outside perspective. This action can create a valuable new inbound link (which helps your search engine positioning), bring in new blog subscribers, and help cement your status as an expert.

# Photography and Video

Traditional travel writing books spend lots of time discussing photography and selling photos. I'm only going to spend a few pages on photography because now it's a given. In the digital age, photos aren't something that are going to earn you much extra cash. They're table stakes. When writing for the web, a story without photos is a half-done assignment.

Think of photography like a college degree in the 21$^{st}$ century. It's nothing special like it was half a century ago. It's something you're expected to have if you're a person trying to get a good job. If you're a travel writer now, you're expected to be able to take decent photos.

Note that I said "decent," not "fantastic." When you're doing a feature story for a magazine, they want fantastic, so they're going to hire a professional photographer. They want a pro who will give them beautiful shots that can dramatically cover two pages. In magazines with smaller budgets, they'll either use photos you submit or they'll pull stock photos of some kind. They want something that looks good in print, but they can't afford to hire a photographer and pay expenses. So they compromise.

When you get to articles on the internet, the visuals just aren't as important. Maybe pad/slate computers will produce a hybrid solution that works, but for now most web publishers avoid large photos with a high resolution. These shots slow down the time it takes a web page to load, plus the dimensions and layout of a web page don't allow for the kind of "spreads" you get in a magazine. Photos just don't have the same impact visually on the web and they certainly don't have much impact on the bottom line for content sites. For better or worse, readers are just in more of a hurry online.

The other problem is, photography has really been devalued in the digital age, the same way routine writing has been devalued. The reasons are similar: anybody can do it, we're awash in far more images than we need, and there's no scarcity. Every year, the entries in amateur travel photography contests get better and better. If nothing else, there's a lot more good stuff to choose from. Everyone's got decent equipment and everyone can take 100 shots of the same subject or scene to get it right without spending any money for photo development.

So it's a rare case that a web editor will pay you much extra for photos. Usually they are a required part of the package. Required to the point that they can make or break your submission. When I asked GoNomad editor Max Hartshorne what freelancers do wrong the most, he went straight to photos. "They don't send good photos, or they send just a few photos when we need at least 20-30 to choose from. They don't put it all in one email with a link." I deal with this myself every week as an editor at Perceptive Travel. Part of the submission process is making things easy for the person on the other end. That means getting the whole package right, not just the Word document.

Here are some tips on making your photo part of the package more attractive and easier to use, whether you are writing for someone else or illustrating your own blog.

## Get a Good Camera

It seems like I shouldn't have to mention this, but I still see writers walking around with the inexpensive camera they bought five years ago. It's hard to take good photos without a good camera. Fortunately the definition of "good" has gotten more fluid. With some skill, it's possible to get good photos with a simple point-and-shoot automatic, as long as the light is good.

Taking one step up will make a noticeable difference, however. There's a category of cameras called "super-zoom" that are better than a basic point-and-shoot but not as heavy, bulky, or complicated as a digital SLR camera. With these you have a long zoom, a larger lens, and manual override controls. For most situations, that's plenty. You can pick one up for between $200 and $500 depending on the zoom length and the bells and whistles included. They're not compact enough to fit in your pocket, but they take better photos, especially when you can't get right up close to the subject.

If you have more money to spend and don't mind lugging around more equipment, a SLR camera will provide the most control, the best lenses, and the most features. I personally don't think it's worth it for most people, but plenty of other writers strongly disagree. Figure out what's right for you.

A small travel tripod can be a big help, especially in low light situations. You can use this with a video camera as well.

## Learn to Take Interesting Shots

If you have never taken a photography course in your life, you might want to sign up now. I've met travelers with great equipment who come back with collections of boring photos. I've met others who use a $75 pocket camera and come back with stunning shots. The first never developed an eye for photography or the skills to compensate for less-than-ideal conditions. The second learned and improved. The first type takes photos when the light is all wrong. The second type takes advantage of periods when the light is just right. The second person overcomes an equipment deficit with an artistic eye, patience, and better framing.

There are some basic skills that can be easily learned and applied. Sure, the pros spend a lifetime honing these skills and developing their own bags of tricks, but for the writer who is not trying to get into *National Geographic*, a basic level of proficiency will do it. So take a class, do online tutorials, read some books on the subject, get advice from others with more skill and experience. As with writing, after you know the basics, the rest of getting better is all about practice and continual improvement.

There are some key strategies that help when taking travel photos for publication, however.

1) **Get some color in the shots.** Travel is about adventure, fantasy, relaxation, fun, excitement, and exploration. Five drab gray shots won't convey any of that.
2) **Mix up the composition.** Leaf through a bunch of magazines and you'll see this aspect over and over again. Some wide scenery shots from afar, some close shots of details. A crowd, then one face. A night shot, a bright beach shot. Think in terms of opposites as you shoot.
3) **We like people!** A travel story with no people in any of the photos looks kind of strange. This can be local people or it can be travelers having fun, but landscapes and monuments alone don't cut it.
4) **Show us something different.** The best photos tell us a story or at least intrigue us enough to make us stop and ponder the image. Don't take the same postcard shot everyone else has taken a hundred times if you want it to be worthy of publication. Look for a unique angle.

## Find the Drama

There are some situations where you are limited in how creative you can be. The obvious one for travel writers is hotels. I've probably published 600 hotel photos and have edited a few thousand more. There's a limit to the variety and it's hard to many any standard room shot dramatic without manipulating it. But still, there's a lot you can do just by shooting from a different angle, framing things in an interesting way, and grabbing images that capture the Golden Mean in design—especially outside of the guest room.

The same principle can be applied to other difficult cases like river rafting trips, hiking trips, or visits to iconic monuments. It's a challenge, but the answers are usually right in front of you if you wander around surveying the scene before snapping away upon arrival. Take your time and explore.

## Learn to Edit

On an almost weekly basis, I'll get a writer sending me giant 4 megabyte photos by e-mail, which is a royal pain in the rear for a web editor. These are photos coming straight out of the writer's camera, files that are so large they could be blown up to wall-covering poster size. For the web, it's like sending me a novel when I've asked for a one-page story. It's the pet peeve that Max Hartshorne immediately thought of at the beginning of this section and you can bet it bugs other editors too. Do you want to risk an editor not hiring you again just because you can't be bothered to figure out how to use simple photo editing software, or figuring out how to upload your shots to Picasa?

Take the time to learn how to crop, how to reduce the resolution, how to sharpen. You don't need the big learning curve and expense of Photoshop for any of this. The software that came with your camera can probably do it. If not there are some free shareware programs that are easy and effective. Two of my favorites are Irfanview and Photo! (yes, with an exclamation point at the end). Get either at download.com.

A so-so photo can be made to look great with the right cropping and a lot of composition problems can be fixed with a few simple tweaks. Learn this stuff so you can turn in decent photos or you can post interesting images on your own blog.

The easiest option of all when writing for someone else is to upload your photos to an online storage system such as Flickr, Picasa, PhotoBucket, or Fokti. Then you can just send a link and the editor can choose and download at will, in some cases with different size options already set up. If you're worried about someone stealing them, you can restrict the access or take them down after the editor is done.

## Shoot some video

Only some sites want video. It hogs bandwidth and doesn't produce much income, but for others it is essential. Few need anything from you that's going to win a short films competition though. A clip of a minute or two is plenty and the resolution just needs to be good enough for the web. Some bloggers use a lot of video because it can tell a story or bring a place alive. Some also like to have their face on camera, so they can function like a travel show host.

Doing this used to be a major expense and hassle, but not anymore. A Flip camera or something similar is "good enough" and is dead simple to use. Most quality still cameras now have built-in video capabilities and some super-zoom point-and-shoots take impressive HD video—starting at a price tag under $250. There is video capability with the latest generation of the iPhone and even the Nano. The quality is not too hot, but if you've watched much on YouTube you've probably realized viewers aren't too concerned about that when viewing on the web. The subject matter is more important.

There's a second step to the shooting though—editing—and it's not as quick or easy as editing a photo. With a few hours of practice you can get it down, with software that's already loaded on your Windows or Mac laptop. It's time-consuming though, something best done when you've got a sizable block of time on your hands, like when on a long flight back home.

If you're serious about doing this on a regular basis, you may want to invest in an external microphone. People are used to putting up with low-quality video, but they don't have much tolerance for low-quality audio. We're starting to see some portable models with shielded mics, so perhaps in the near future this will become standard.

# The Craft of Travel Writing

*Easy reading is damn hard writing.*
– Nathaniel Hawthorne

Anyone can claim to be a writer. Most aren't good enough at it to make a living from that assertion.

There are plenty of courses, books, and seminars out there that will teach you how to be a great writer. Some are decent, some are great, others are a waste of time.

I have to admit I've never taken a writing course or workshop of any kind, apart from the usual high school and college courses that seemed to give me enough to get started. Mostly I learned by reading a lot and writing a lot, on a wide range of subjects. This takes longer and I probably could have benefitted from a few intense workshops in the beginning, but in my opinion practice is more valuable than just learning techniques. You need a good base of knowledge, you need to have at least a modicum of talent, and then the rest is a matter of getting better and better at the craft.

Some people get a lot of value out of courses and seminars though, because if nothing else that provides dedicated writing time with no distractions plus valuable feedback from the instructor and peers. In these courses writers learn to drop some bad

> *No matter how smart you are, you're not going to be very good for a few years at least. I don't know why exactly this is true, but it is. Everyone's a little cheesy at first, a little overwritten, a lot cliché. It takes a tremendous amount of practice not to be. Most people never get there.*
>
> - Lena Katz freelance writer and author

habits and pick up some new good ones.

Some writing courses and seminars are taught by respected editors and writers who have proven beyond a doubt that they know what's great writing and what's not. You can find out more about these in the resources section at the end.

There are also some really fine books out there on becoming a better writer. Some are focused on travel, like the highly-recommended *Travel Writing* book out on Lonely Planet, edited by former *San Francisco Chronicle* travel editor Don George. Others cover creative non-fiction in general and provide inspiration and instruction for going from average to terrific.

The one drawback to these books and courses is that they mostly focus on feature writing: on long magazine narratives where the author has plenty of space to let loose and be creative. That's all well and good, but since this book is about the commercial aspect of writing, I have to warn you that this is only one slice of the travel writing pie and it's not one that's getting any bigger.

> *Again and again, we editors come up with stories we'd like to assign...only to struggle to pinpoint the best freelancer to write them. Editors treasure any writer who communicates well (by asking questions and providing updates), meets their deadlines, stays within their word-count limits, conforms to the publication's style, and works at a fair market rate. I generally find that freelancers break down into two categories, the stylists and the reporters. Stylists write gracefully and absorbingly. Reporters get the facts straight and plug all of the potential logical holes in their pieces (such as being sure to answer one of the Who What Where When Why type of questions).*
>
> *Keep in mind which category you fall into, if either one tends to apply. Then agree to do assignments that will allow you to play to your strengths and showcase your skills, be it reporting or writing stylishly. Of course, you may be one of the exceptional writers who is a master of both skills, in which case, please get in touch with me so I can learn a thing or two from you.*
>
> – Sean O'Neill, Senior Editor, *Budget Travel*

I always thought editors were exaggerating when they talked about off-target pitches, query letters punctuated with spelling errors, and god-awful stories they had to sift through week after week.

Then I became an editor.

Man oh man are there some bad writers out there. Setting aside the problem that way to many writers are lazy about reading guidelines (or think the guidelines apply to everyone but them), plenty of people who call themselves writers should really sign up for one of those writing seminars or buy a few books on how to write. Some of them appear to have not even passed high school English class.

So before we get into the finer points of craft and skill, do you have the basics down? Can you spell? Do you understand subject/verb agreement and the difference between an adjective and an adverb? Do you know the difference between active and passive voice? Do you understand when to use a colon and when to use a semicolon?

If not, please go get schooled before you send off a single query or start a blog. Get *The Elements of Style* and study it cover to cover, then read then read *The Elephants of Style* for some more tempered advice. Read *Eats, Shoots, and Leaves.* Figure out the differences between British and American English in spelling and punctuation if you want to submit stories to editors outside your home country. Ask for the *Chicago Manual of Style* for your next holiday or birthday present or reference it in the library.

When you have a spelling or grammar question, don't just guess. Look it up so you'll know. We're spoiled rotten for information now: you don't have to drive to the library to find the proper uses of racked, wracked, or wrecked. So if you send in a sloppy query, it broadcasts that you're too lazy to even do a Google search. Game over.

I learned a secret long ago that may have been the biggest factor in my success: showing up and doing what you promised impresses people more than virtuosity. People who do the hiring in any industry love finding someone they can depend on.

Don't think you have to be the most talented, the most outrageous, or the most technically gifted to be a successful writer. Often you just have to be reasonably good at what you're doing and be able to meet the requirements, whatever they may be. There are lots of actors making a good living without being "movie stars." They show up on time, they know their lines, they hit their marks, they get hired again.

It's a similar scene with most creative endeavors. Movies love to glamorize the strung-out manic-depressant tortured artist and there's some anecdotal evidence that being a genius and being unhinged go hand-in-hand, but the unhinged often die young. Keep living and be merely great instead. Strangers won't cry at your grave, but you'll actually live to see kids or nieces who know you.

Beyond the fundamentals, to say what's good or bad writing we first have to look at the changing definition of what "good writing" even means. First it means considering the intermediary customer (who is hiring you) or the end customer—the reader.

## Narrative Feature Writing

*A magazine that speaks to readers, transforms them and transports them either to a place they'd like to live or like to travel, that's the best of print journalism. Solving a problem is good, but transporting and transforming is the goal of all good editors.*
– Eleanor Griffin, Editor in Chief, *Southern Living*

Narrative feature writing is what most everyone imagines themselves doing when they hear "travel writer." All those multi-page features with beautiful photos that are splashed across several pages, your byline in bold type at the top, right under the title. Creative, evocative writing that brings a destination to life and explores characters that glide across the stage of your week or more in the region.

Well, good luck with that. Those assignments are out there, but for magazines especially the assignments mostly go to veterans with a long track record. Narrative feature assignments are like starring roles in a movie: sometimes they go to unknowns, but usually the editor wants a proven pro. Nobody gets in trouble that way.

It is a little easier to get narratives published on the web since there are far more outlets—some quite prestigious now, some visited by only a handful of readers on a regular basis. Gregory Hubbs of TransitionsAbroad.com hosts an annual narrative travel writing contest that pulls in some surprisingly great features from relative unknowns. He says, "A travel narrative which is well-written is inspiring and interesting, especially when it rises to the level of literature or universal experience, and the web offers many the opportunity to contribute substantive thoughts and work."

Learning to write well along the way over time will get you ready for these assignments or contests when they come, so jump at any chance you get to do these kinds of stories. Write for small magazines, write for webzines, write without worrying about the money. Then by the time you graduate from the minor leagues to the majors, you'll be ready to hit a home run.

To get good at this kind of writing, you need more talent than for any of the other types that follow. You need the tools of a novelist, the eyes of a journalist, and the general knowledge that comes from a never-ending education and a natural curiosity about the world around you—and its history. For this type of writing, you can't just fire off a draft you wrote in one sitting.

I've won quite a few awards for my narrative writing and I choose stories for Perceptive Travel that often show up in "best travel writing" anthologies, so I think I have a pretty good sense about what's required to be good at this. I couldn't have put out the stories that won these awards when I started out as a freelance writer though. I wasn't good enough yet.

Some writers have more natural talent than I do and success comes faster. Catch them in an honest moment, however, and every one will tell you they edit and re-edit, they still get advice from others, and they still occasionally get the feeling that what they've put on the page is sub-par. One of the writers I respect the most once said quietly, "I still feel like a hack sometimes."

If you don't feel that sometimes, you're probably not stretching enough. Writing a compelling travel narrative that will keep people reading for 2,000 or 4,000 words takes real work. Don't let any direct-mail come-on that promises great success after one weekend tell you differently.

> *I want a writer who can grab me from the beginning of a pitch or story, with a vivid image or a compelling scene or wordplay. I want a writer who can keep me hooked, who can bring me deep into a story. I want a writer who understands how to structure and tell a story, who knows what to put in the story and also what to leave out. I want clarity. I want a writer with an eye for detail, someone who can bring me into a scene or a place. I want to be entertained. I want a writer who, by the end of the story, has made me feel something or taught me something that I didn't know.*
>
> – Michael Yessis, co-founder and co-editor-in-chief, WorldHum.com

It's not hard to find good examples of narrative writing, so I'm not going to take the usual page-padding route of posting examples in this book. You can find them in annual travel writing anthologies or compilations put out by the likes of Travelers' Tales and Seal Press. You can find them in magazines that strive to rise above the rest, in non-travel magazines like *Esquire*, the *Atlantic*, *New York Times Magazine*, or *Men's Journal*. Usually there's at least one good feature in the big travel magazines themselves, especially *National Geographic Traveler, Outpost, Wanderlust, and Afar*. You can find them in webzines that include good narratives on a regular basis, such as Perceptive Travel and World Hum.

You can also see the elements of a good narrative article by reading the ones that win contests. It's all up to the whims of the judges, of course, but see what came out on top and compare it to what you just wrote. Is yours as gripping, as wrenching, as exhilarating, or as funny—whichever one applies? If not, keep editing.

# Short F.O.B. ("Front of Book) Features

Flip through any magazine on any subject at your local newsstand and you'll find that there is a far larger market for short capsule articles of a page or less than there is for long stories. The average magazine story is now well under 500 words, that average dragged down by all the cutesy little one-paragraph nuggets that have only become more common as attention spans have shortened.

This is where the work is. If you want to break in as a freelancer at a magazine, get good at saying what needs to be said in 400 words and then getting out. If your idea can't be captured in a capsule story like this, then rethink the angle. If you can come up with ideas that fit into small boxes over and over again, you will get repeat assignments. Do it enough times for one editor and you build trust. With trust you can finally pitch those full-blown ideas that require you spending a week in the Andes or rafting down some obscure river on the other side of the world.

The writing for these short pieces is very different than for long ones. This is where you really need to study the publication to get a feel for their style. In general though, you're required to be crisp, efficient, and have a bag full of puns at your disposal. What you write will often sound much like what every other person writes in that issue—or more correctly, everyone end up sounds like the editor. It's a formula and it's annoying, but apparently it works.

For these articles, the idea is to catch someone's eye as they're flipping through the magazine and to present something in bite-sized form. This may be something new, something noteworthy, something odd, or something funny. In any case, it's an article that gets the point across without a lot of exposition. This is probably the only kind of writing I can think of where being good at Twitter is actually useful for something. If you can get your point across in short, catchy sentences, you'll be a good match for this kind of work.

# Service Article Writing

The columns Wendy Perrin writes for *Condé Nast Traveler* are nothing like the cutesy, trend-focused F.O.B. short pieces in the magazine, nor are they anything like the denser narrative features that make a destination come alive. The same goes for the useful articles written by Christopher Elliott for *National Geographic Traveler*. These two respected columnists are writing "service" pieces every issue—articles meant to inform and guide travelers, articles designed to eliminate hassles, save people money, and help them make good decisions.

As much as we writers get thrilled about big sweeping destination stories, most readers are checking out travel magazines and websites to learn how to travel better or cheaper. Service articles are where it's at, in magazines that cover nothing but travel and magazines that only cover it now and then. The latter would include magazines like *Smart Money, Real Simple, Every Day with Rachel Ray, Women's Day, Men's Journal, Newsweek*, or a hundred others that only cover travel as another lifestyle aspect.

In print or on the web, this is where the bulk of the assignments are. So while many travel writing articles and books seem almost obsessively focused on the craft of capturing the essence of a place and engaging the senses, what most travel writers sell on a regular basis has nothing to do with all that. People read magazines for enjoyment and escape, yes, but more often they read them to learn something or get ideas to make them richer/more attractive/more successful/happier. Editors know this and therefore they cram the front third or half of the magazine full of service articles. If you don't believe me, start making a list of how many pieces in any magazine you pick up start with some variation of "How to..." or "Tips."

This is even more true on the web, where people land on pages after a search meant to answer a specific question. "What are the cheapest hostels in Prague?" "How do I catch a bus from Cancun to Merida?" "How do I get a visa for India?" "How much will it cost to rent a house for a week in Myrtle Beach?" The people doing these searches want an expert to give them definitive answers to their questions. They don't really care about the fluff.

If you run your own blog or website, answering these questions over and over builds an audience. Let's say someone lands on your site to find out an answer to the Google search, "campground costs Smoky Mountains." If you provide that information and your site seems both authoritative and in line with their interests, that reader may stick around and keep browsing. The person may bookmark the site or recommend it to others through social media. Over time, this builds up subscribers and followers. A long blog post talking about your boring camping trip near Gatlinburg does not.

Service articles are the heart of travel writing. So become an expert on some topic or destination and you'll get work telling readers what you know.

## Web Feature Writing

Feature writing for internet sites is different than writing for print media, mostly because the attention span is even shorter on the web. Numerous studies have shown people read faster and with less attention as soon as they go on the web. Also, much of the difference depends on word count. Perceptive Travel, World Hum, Transitions Abroad, and GoNomad publish relatively long articles. They toss aside the idea that everything has to be in easily digested chunks and they have differentiated themselves from the crowd by doing so.

Most websites aim for shorter pieces though, rarely topping 1,000 words. For search engine optimization purposes, they would rather have a focused story of 400 to 600 words clearly utilizing specific keyword phrases than to have a long murkier narrative with subplots and characters.

In general, the higher the pay, the harder it is for a newcomer to break into a given web publication, but it's still easier online than with print since the publishing constraints come from available budgets, not from issue thickness or the ratio of full-page ads to articles.

# Short Web Article Writing

See the blog section below for blog posts, but there are many travel websites out there that pay for short articles on a specific subject. These are sometimes meant to offer complete destination coverage on a specific region, so the editor will assign short pieces on each town or attraction and will put each one on its own page. Or a site may require unique hotel reviews, unique restaurant reviews, boutique store rundowns, etc.

More often than not, the editor cares more about the uniqueness and the presence of the right keywords than about how well you have crafted the story. Punctuate properly and use good grammar and you're set. In other cases (such as the hotel reviews assigned at LuxuryLatinAmerica.com), the editor wants what's on the page to be better and more detailed than anything else out there. Again, study the publication and guidelines carefully to turn one assignment into many.

For these stories, you may be required to submit them in HTML-ready text as well, or be required to post them through a dashboard and manually insert all links and photos. I advise you to learn all this anyway as you'll need the skills in the future.

# Blog Writing

There's a fine line between travel content sites and blogs (originally called "weblogs"), but a blog is expected to be in a specific format of current posts on the front page and others accessed by category and/or tag links.

There are two kinds of blog writing: what you write for your own and what you write for someone else. For your own, you make the rules, so I'm not going to tell you how or what to write. It pays off in the long run though to look like a professional: edit, proof, spell-check, and don't use others' photos without the proper permission or attribution. Be unique instead of just copying or commenting on what others have written. Offer something worth returning to. Write around a certain theme or point of view instead of regularly posting about your cat, your husband, politics, and your weekend getaway all on one blog (unless you are a celebrity and people really care). Write on a reasonably regular schedule.

Most people visit blogs to be entertained, to learn something, to get advice, to improve their life, or to keep up on a specific subject. If you don't meet one of those needs, your traffic will probably never take off.

Writing for blogs is very different than writing articles that are meant to be more permanent. Blog posts are expected to be less formal and more conversational, with shorter and fewer paragraphs. This doesn't mean you can't write a 2,000-word diatribe now and then, but don't make it a daily habit. You can write things on blogs that nobody would publish—and you might get a lot of traffic.

You can drill down to a level of detail that wouldn't get past an editor's desk at a magazine. I've done posts on water purifiers, the south Florida Tri-Rail system, and the price of rum in Guatemala on my Cheapest Destinations blog. On the Perceptive Travel blog, the writers there have done posts on the Willie Nelson Truck Stop, the Hutchinson Kansas Grain Elevator, and travelers dealing with fashion snobs in Europe. Your editorial limits are far more broad on a blog, so go nuts.

> *For the most part I think blogging will continue to be a slightly less digested form of writing than formal journalism or essay writing. In most cases, including mine, it bears as many similarities to letter writing as it does to journalism. And just like authors from years past approached letter writing with a different focus than essay writing, there's a similar difference with blog writing. There's simply less rewriting and polishing to be done with a blog entry.*
>
> – Rolf Potts, in TransitionsAbroad.com

If you're getting paid to write for someone else's blog, naturally you need to adhere to their requirements. They all have specific content needs and unique dashboard interfaces, plus an editorial style of their own that you need to match. Guest posts for others' blogs need to blend in with their existing style and format.

I love writing for blogs more than other formats because it's where I feel I can say exactly what I want. I like the immediacy of it and the ability to follow any whim in terms of subject matter. When readers stop by, it's because of content I've created, not because of what an army of editors and writers has collectively put together. But don't be fooled: it's still a lot of work though, especially if you're doing multiple posts every week—or every day. The nice side effect? You get a lot of practice with coming up with ideas and writing about them.

## Trade Writing

Writing for trade publications essentially means writing for a non-consumer audience. You are writing in a factual and comprehensive style for people in the business. They are reading what you wrote because they need to for their job, not because they are spending a leisurely afternoon being entertained.

Over the years, I've done a lot of work for two publications sold through subscription to travel agents. One specializes in detailed hotel reviews and the other specialized in mini-guidebook reports that summarize a destination and give travel agents info they can package into a report for customers. One of my first real gigs as a travel writer was one of these, writing reviews of 79 top hotels scattered around Turkey. I did well on that, so they hired me to do Israel, Egypt, Jordan, Korea, Guam, Saipan, Nepal, and India within the next three years. I went on to cover Peru, Argentina, and parts of Mexico and the U.S. I still work for them today. I love these jobs because the terms are clear, the pay is decent, and they pay on time. Business to business writing is often like that—more professional and more stable.

I know other writers who get most of their income from trade magazines such as *Travel Weekly* or *Meetings and Incentives*. In general this kind of writing requires more industry knowledge than most beginners have, however, so this is one of the few freelance jobs where the editor may ask for a resume or a rundown on your work history.

Trade publications writing is more journalistic than most travel writing. Business readers want the facts and supporting quotes without a lot of fluff. They won't look at your byline and don't want your opinion. The hotel and destination reports I've written didn't even provide a byline: I'm anonymous. Writing for the trades is about the paycheck, not about getting famous or building up a following.

## Guidebook Writing

Are you obsessive about the facts? Detail-oriented? Super-organized? A fast writer? Let's hope so on all counts if you want to be a guidebook writer. This is a Job with a capital "J." I get stressed out just thinking about all the work that goes into creating a guidebook and my wife has standing orders to talk me out of it should I ever be offered a contract to write one.

I admire guidebook writers because they have serious dedication. One project requires months to a year of their life and in order to make the finances work, they have to do it quickly, thoroughly, and efficiently. Every time they have to defy the old handyman question of, "Do you want it done quick, cheap, or well? Pick two."

How far you can flex in the writing depends greatly on the publisher, but in any case your verbal skills take a back seat to a guidebook's core purpose: supplying information. You can embellish the descriptions and add a dose of humor, but not until you've got the current bus schedule worked out in detail, thank you very much. Apart from a few boxed sections that allow you to tell a story about some specific site or historical event, you barely have time to write full sentences before moving on to the requisite restaurant listings and museum hours.

Some writers thrive in this environment and are masters at getting everything just right. Others quickly get into the right mode for a guidebook, but then branch off and do wonderful narrative articles as well. In Zora O'Neill's case, a cookbook even.

There are very few courses or books for this kind of writing. Your best teachers are other writers, the publisher's instructions, and stacks of guidebooks studied in detail. For the dark side of the story, read Thomas Kohnstamm's book *Do Travel Writers Go to Hell?* Then go read all the rebuttals from other guidebook writers by searching the name of that book on Google. They won't be hard to find.

## Travel Book Writing

Not all travel books are guidebooks. Some of the best-selling ones are something else: narratives from the likes of Bill Bryson J. Maarten Troost, Paul Theroux, Frances Mayes, or Tim Cahill. Some are informational books on a specific subject, such as traveling with children or gaming the frequent flyer system. Others are reference books on niches such as responsible travel or are coffee table books filled with gorgeous photos.

So it's impossible to generalize except to say you need to know enough about that subject to sustain a whole book's worth of text. You need to be an accomplished writer with plenty to say. And if it's a narrative book, you had better be able to tell a great story and have a good following on top of that. Otherwise an agent won't sign you and you're stuck putting it out yourself—a daunting prospect for something that's not informational in nature.

If you have aspirations of writing a book, do your homework on how to put together a good proposal, outline your book, and then make the magic happen for 250+ pages. I'll just emphasize this one point: before you decide to write a book, make sure you can write a lot of good articles or a few years' worth of blog posts. The book—and the marketing—will come much easier after that.

> *Writers must first be good writers, they must know their subjects, and if I'm going to consider them for writing or editing a book they have to be personable and flexible. Life is too short to work with someone you don't like or respect, especially on a creative project that requires collaboration. They also need to be responsible and reliable, so I know they're going to do what we've agreed they will do.*
>
> – Larry Habegger, Executive Editor, Travelers' Tales Publishing

# Perks and Profit

As many a travel writer will say, "The money sucks, but the perks are great."

Let's be real—this is why many otherwise frustrated writers stick with it. If they stopped writing, they would be forced to travel less. And they would travel in a different way if they had to pay for every aspect of every trip themselves. Goodbye pampering resort, hello Motel 6.

Working as a travel writer and having some success at it leads to that list of perks the come-on travel writing seminars tout so loudly: free flights, free hotel rooms, nice dinners, and then a big tax write-off for expenses you still end up footing yourself.

The line between "free" and "business expense" is a blurry one though, so it's not really free if you're working the whole time instead of enjoying the experience as much as you would on vacation. It's not uncommon for a travel writer to be working for 12 hours straight for days on end, running around fact-checking and typing on a laptop while everyone around them is kicking back and having fun. It's not uncommon for press trip itineraries to start at 8 a.m. and not finish until after a late dinner.

Still, a week working on a Caribbean island beats a week behind a desk any day, so most writers bitch a lot but keep doing it.

People perceived as "influencers" get lots of perks, so become one and you get showered. That's true whether you are a fashion writer getting clothes, a music writer getting concert tickets, or an a golf writer puttering a cart down a new course each week. In an ironic twist, it's also true for rich celebrities, who get much of what they wear and use without paying anything.

Personally, I'm fine with all this, but be aware that some people aren't, including the editors at some traditional media outlets. Always be aware of how these offerings and their influence on your writing will be perceived. If you're a shill for hire and are not honest in your writings as a result of what you have received, you may not be taken seriously as a writer—or a person.

I feel that a travel writer on assignment is compromised in so many ways already that the various "truth in travel" variations on a slogan are mere marketing no matter what. Whether the magazine is paying your expenses or the tourism board is paying your expenses doesn't make much difference in the end. Either way, it's not coming out of your pocket. Plus you're not going to see a scathing negative hotel review make it past the editor either way. Good luck finding any kind of investigative journalism or muckraking in the travel press from any publication that depends on advertising from the industry to make a living. "Don't bite the hand that feeds you" is a maxim for survival no matter who is paying your bar bill.

So I have no qualms about going on press trips (also called "fam trips"—for "familiarization") or accepting hosting from airlines, hotels, or tourism boards. Most readers of my articles or books would have a really hard time figuring out which trips were sponsored and which were paid for by the publication. Or which ones I paid for myself while on vacation. If you possess things like morals, ethics, and a conscious, it's usually not much of an issue. There are terms for writers who don't possess these things: they're generally referred to as hacks, whores, or shills. Try not to be one of these.

It's hard to turn down any offer that starts with, "We would like to fly you to…" but sometimes you have to take a breath and say no. Free travel is a beautiful thing, but remember that you're trying to be a writer that earns money, not a prostitute who writes.

# About Those Press Trips…

"I really have no patience for RUDE journalists! I don't care how many million subscribers, you have! Rudeness is unnecessary!"

That was what a PR person posted for a thousand of her Twitter followers to see after I sent an impatient reply to her e-mail one day.

I'm generally not known as a guy who is hard to get along with, but the exchange had gotten testy for a good reason.

Here's the preceding message from her, what had caused me to get ticked off enough to be rude.

"I want to let you know that if [nearby Mexican resort area] is going to be a piece of your story—then I can probably tell you that we won't be able to help with airfare, just because if [the resort area I represent] sponsors it, they won't want to be mentioned in the same article as [that other nearby resort area]."

I replied that it seemed a bit ridiculous to make that demand considering that every single guidebook already lumped the whole region together anyway, both areas are served by the same airport, and, really, um, are you kidding me?! I had offered this person five confirmed media placements and she was worried about whether I might mention her client's kid sister to the south. I ended up scrapping all five assignments—plus the multiple blog entries that would also have come out of the trip—and packed my bag for another destination instead.

This is just one example of the kind of ethical minefield you navigate in travel journalism. Just putting "travel" and "journalism" in the same sentence is in itself a minefield. Let's face it: if you were a real journalist you would be working for a news organization covering night court battles, garbage worker strikes, political corruption, or school board elections. Instead you're covering what people do with a week or two of leisure time. That's akin to writing about movies, celebrities, music, TV shows, or designer furniture. With skill you can make it verbal art worth reading, but it's not going to win you a Pulitzer Prize for great journalism.

The person who writes the exposé on the amount of garbage your average cruise ship generates or the amount of electricity wasted by your average luxury hotel is not going to get a lot of future assignments from the travel industry press. No matter how many "truth in travel" or "honest recommendation" proclamations the travel magazines and newspaper sections may put in their slogans, they are clearly a mouthpiece for the industry. An always-positive mouthpiece.

There's a very good reason you don't see scathing negative hotel reviews or stories about disappointing trips in these publications. Their goal is to sell a fantasy that their advertisers will love. Every trip is wonderful. Every place is fantastic. A place may have been bad in the past, but now it is "on the rise" or "the place to go this year." Free trips or not, there is no room for real honesty in most travel publications, especially in the print world where so much revenue is at stake. If Celebrity Cruises is paying you $50,000 an issue for their ad placements, do you really want to run a feature story on how cruise ships are hotbeds for viruses and food poisoning? If Marriott is essentially paying you your nice editor's salary, are you really going to green-light a funny story about how the Marriott rooms in Lima have the same bedspreads as the Marriott rooms in Los Angeles and Lisbon? Of course not. It's career suicide. Leave that to the bloggers. They've got nothing to lose.

## The Ups and Downs of Press Trips

Still, spend any time on any kind of travel writing message boards and you will find heated arguments about the ethics of accepting freebies, especially in the U.S. I find this really comical since you almost never see the same arguments coming from people who write about music, cars, golf, movies, wine, or fashion. They don't think twice about getting everything they write about for free and being wined and dined on a regular basis. "What, you expect me to pay for all this myself? Out of my income? No way, it's my *job*!"

When I worked for RCA Records in Nashville and New York, I had more than a few party-til-dawn crazy nights with music writers from the likes of *Rolling Stone* and the *New York Times*. I'm talking limos, backstage parties, free-flowing cocktails, and drugs I'd never seen before and haven't seen since. More than once, the bastard would still write about how crappy our band was on stage that night. But hey, it was publicity and nobody expected that writer to suddenly love our overhyped band just because he was licking some kind of elicit powder off a model's tummy and got a limo ride to the show. It was the relationship that mattered. We wanted his attention on a regular basis and we got it. He had a good time and always returned our calls.

For some reason though, in travel there are more than a few holier-than-thou editors and self-appointed ethical experts who feel that no travel writer can get a free hotel room night without it clouding his judgment, that nobody can write honestly about a destination if someone from the destination covered her plane ticket to get there.

In my two decades of experience, this just isn't supported by the reality of what gets printed. I once got so annoyed with someone who took this stance that I sent her 20 of my hotel reviews for a certain city and challenged her to determine which hotels had hosted me and which ones I had simply toured and reviewed without staying. She flunked miserably, getting one of the hosted ones right out of five and guessing that four had put me up that really had not.

Press trips and hosted stays are probably as old as travel writing itself. Just look at the marketing value of "George Washington slept here!" or "As seen in The Odyssey!" The first thing I would do if I opened a new hotel would be to put together a list of travel writers I wanted to invite. It's far cheaper and more effective than getting the word out through advertising. Destinations with huge budgets put a lot of money into bringing writers in on press trips and destinations with tiny budgets still do everything they can to at least get writers in the area involved in getting them some press.

If you've ever wondered why you suddenly see a place like Dubai or Croatia featured in seemingly every publication you pick up, here's why: they spent a lot of money luring in writers and they spent a lot of money advertising in the big magazines to influence them to send their own writers. (Sometimes this is a clear tit-for-tat arrangement, sometimes it's more subtle, but over time you'll see a clear correlation between the advertising and the editorial coverage in most large magazines.)

If you're honest and a good writer, it shouldn't matter whether the magazine paid, the tourism bureau paid, or you paid. Some people aren't honest though, and some are just whores. They'll write anything the hosting company wants them to write. It'll be a boring story, everything will be flattering, and there will be very little conflict or depth. This is what gives rise to the derogatory term "press trip story."

On the other hand, if you're a skilled writer who speaks the truth, you can still get a great story out of a press trip, provided it's not crammed tight with irrelevant stops and there's at least a smidgen of free time to go get some color and some quotes. I've won multiple writing awards from stories that have come out of press trips or individually sponsored trips, as many as I've won from situations where I paid my own way, frankly. Many successful writers I have hired over the years as an editor can say the same.

The key to making this work and to retain some integrity is to find a real angle. What would you write about no matter who is paying? What aspect really interests you personally? Where's the personal connection to your background or history—or that of your travel companion or family that is along?

## *Press Trips and Online Media*

Once upon a time, press trips were a simple affair. Public relations people and CVB (convention and visitors bureau) people knew exactly who to invite. They made a few calls to their A list (magazine editors and major newspaper editors), they then made a few calls to their B list (reliable freelancers and newsletter editors), and the invite list was done. Later as staff positions dried up and some publications got all high and mighty about appearing to be neutral, freelancers got more invites.

Then everything turned upside down when new media took over. As newspapers became irrelevant in the travel world and some blogs started pulling in more readers than your average print magazine, some (but still not all) travel tourism people started to wise up. They invited multi-outlet influencers instead of print editors with a specific circulation and they saw a flood of new visitors to their website. A year later, they were still getting press out of it.

Now that many websites have far more impact on where people go and where they stay than print publications ever did, public relations people are struggling and flailing when putting together their lists. They know that some writers have a much bigger influence than others, but it's harder to measure that when you don't have easy benchmarks like circulation numbers and full-page ad values.

There are still benchmarks, of course, but they are different. Now it's about traffic, Alexa rank, search engine positioning, inbound links, and "follower" numbers as measured by RSS subscribers and Twitter followers. Obviously this is more complicated and takes more effort to research, but in the end the criteria are the same. How much influence does this person have on potential travelers? How many people read what this person has to say?

Some people are shoo-ins and they get more press trip invites than they can ever accept. Magazine editors, famous bloggers, and freelancers that are regulars at top-tier magazines or websites have to pick and choose which trips they will accept. Fortunately I'm in that category myself now, but wasn't until new media started becoming a force that couldn't be ignored. Up to about early 2008, I'd frequently see press trip invites with a qualifier that I needed to have an assignment from "a print publication with a circulation over 100,000." Never mind that I could get an assignment from a website that reached four or five times that many people every month and the article would keep generating clicks for years. I'd get turned down in favor of a writer from a mid-market newspaper that nobody under 60 is reading anymore.

Other writers struggle to get onto any press trip at all, anywhere. Their freelance assignments are all over the map and each time they have to query anew with a story idea—along with everyone else trying to get an assignment for the same trip. Or they write for some small newspaper or website with very few readers and the people paying for the trip feel the press payoff isn't sufficient. Remember, this is at heart a business transaction. The publicity you will generate must have a value greater than what the host is laying out in expenses. Otherwise, it doesn't add up.

Most travel writers that have been at this for any length of time fall somewhere in between. If they've found a good niche they'll get invited on trips that tie in nicely. If they have a track record at specific publications or blogs that matter, they'll get invited on trips fairly regularly.

## Sponsorship and Individual Hosting

For the sake of the story, being hosted on an individual basis is far preferable to a group press trip. In this arrangement the host covers some or all expenses and/or a hotel hosts you because you are writing about them. Your schedule is your own and you have plenty of time to do real research, focusing on just your angle(s).

Besides the whole ethical quandary this potentially raises with the hosting though, there's the problem that the hosting company or person may still feel completely justified in monopolizing your time and controlling parts of your schedule. In *Smile While You're Lying*, Chuck Thompson says, "One of the problems with accepting comps at swanky resorts is that you end up paying for them with dinners so boring they leave you wanting to scrape your own face off with a souvenir conch shell."

Most narrative feature writers cringe at the idea of a group press trip, being herded around in a van and having everything served up on a fast-moving itinerary. They much prefer to get part of the trip covered, like airfare and some hotel nights, and then have a loose schedule that allows more exploration and interviewing. In these cases it's not a matter of an invite landing in an e-mail box, but rather the writer proposing an individual trip to the right tourism bureau contact or commercial enterprise.

Some writers have success with a third way: going on a group press trip, but tacking a few extra days on the end for individual research. In many cases your contact will go along with this, especially if all that's required is a different date on the plane ticket and you're on your own for expenses on the extra days.

Be advised that individual hosting requires a solid assignment (you may be asked for an assignment letter from an editor), a blog or site with major traffic, or a great track record that shows you will deliver. No tourism bureau person wants to lay out a thousand dollars or more on a risky bet. They want a sure thing. If you can deliver many sure things—as in four or five articles from that one trip—even better. They'll be happy to hear from you again in the future

## How to Get In On This Action

If you do want to go on press trips—and there are a lot of very good reasons to avoid them remember—it is largely out of your hands. Most writers who go on these hosted trips are invited. That's the key word—"invited." Lists of who is going are often filled out before anyone else gets wind that a trip is even happening. The higher the price tag, the higher the standards. So a regional food festival you can drive to may be easy to get in on. A luxury safari tour to Africa though? Much, much tougher.

Sometimes it just seems like blind luck and a lot of it does come down to relationships, but overall the writers invited on press trips are invited because they can deliver an audience that is attractive to the person laying out the money. If the writer's work isn't worth more than the cost to host them, they usually won't be on the list.

So the best way to get invited on trips is to make a name for yourself in one of two ways. The first is to own a niche, meaning you can deliver a very targeted readership. If you have the highest-ranking website for dude ranches in the American West, you're pretty likely to get invites to dude ranch press trips (but not much else, unfortunately). If you are known as the person who gets the most articles published about Croatia, you won't have any problem getting on the list for trips to Croatia.

The other way is to get known for delivering, whatever the subject may be. This goes back to that idea of getting other things published in a variety of outlets. I've been invited to Iceland, South Africa/Botswana, Thailand, Colombia, Honduras, Panama, British Columbia, and a bunch of places in the U.S. and Mexico—for a start. Out of those trips have come articles for a dozen different publications with a wide variety of slants. In most cases, I delivered three or four different pieces from each trip. The PR people loved me, I made a bit of money on my side for the investment in time, and for the most part I managed to put out work I was proud of. I had a blast too. So when writers pooh-pooh press trips as never lending themselves to a good story, I can point to my experience and say, "Well, it depends..."

Now I don't have much trouble getting onto trip lists and if I call with a proposal for a custom individual trip, I can usually get something worked out—assuming there's any money there in the budget and the PR person is not some ditzy recent college grad who doesn't know which way is up. Neither is always a given, so understand that sometimes you will not be hosted in the place where you want to go, no matter how much you plead and how big the opportunity may be. When there's no money, there's no money. This is especially true for airfare, which these days must usually be paid for out of the tourism bureau's budget. Most airlines are incredibly stingy now and they know they are so hated by consumers that they don't even bother trying to get positive press anymore. So if you can pay to fly there yourself or if the place is in driving distance, you'll find the tourism board people to be much more receptive to your requests.

So how would those requests work out? I got a question about this specifically when I was asking on my blog what aspiring travel writers wanted to know, so here's a sample letter you can modify to suit your needs. The idea of this is to show, in no uncertain terms, what you can deliver. Crass as it may be, this is a business transaction. They give you something, you give them something, and hopefully everyone is happy.

**Typical Hosted Individual Trip Proposal**

Dear Key Contact,

I am a freelance travel writer who has contributed to xxx, yyy, and zzz and I am interested in visiting [location] to write a story about [angle] for [publication]. [Information on why this area appeals to you, your connection with it.]

I would be interested in coming [time frame] for x days and would like to explore [explanation of suitable activities].

To put this story together, I am looking for press hosting in terms of [list what is needed such as airfare from your city, hotel nights, admission tickets, and meals]. I expect to place [list expected story length and publication(s)].

I am open to suggestions on making this story great and look forward to your input.

You can see a sampling of other things I have written at [insert portfolio site] and I would be glad to discuss specifics on the phone at your convenience.

I look forward to visiting [location] and sharing my experience with [circulation/monthly visitor number] readers.

There are several potential outcomes to this e-mail. The first is that you are ignored. In that case you should follow up by e-mail in a week then by phone after that to see if they are ignoring you, if the answer is no, or if the e-mail never made it through.

The second outcome is that you are denied. Try to find out why because it may be the publication, it may be you, it may be a lack of money in the budget.

The third is a maybe, dependent on you fulfilling some other requirement (such as an assignment letter), changing your dates, spending less time there, or staying at the state park lodge instead of the Ritz Carlton.

The best outcome is a yes, and then you start working out the details. If you get a yes, make sure both of you are clear on what will be provided. After the trip, stay in touch and be sure you come through with your end of the deal. This doesn't mean writing that everything is lovely when it's really not and ignoring every urge to make a negative observation. As long as you're honest and your comments are based in fact, you can't get criticized for negativity. What it does mean is that you deliver on what you promised. Get the story done and get it published.

I take pride in the fact I have *never* gone on a trip or accepted some kind of hosting that didn't result in at least one story placement. To me, taking a hosted trip without delivering any press is just plain slimy and there are very few cases where that writer who didn't keep up their end of the bargain can be considered anything other than a moocher. Even if that magazine you were writing for went under or the newspaper canceled its assignment after the fact, you should not let that story go. There are plenty of other outlets out there that will publish your story—if the angle is any good. So hunt around and find one, regardless of the pay. Rework the slant if necessary. Otherwise you will lose respect and get blacklisted in a hurry. Just as travel writers talk amongst themselves, so do PR agency people and visitors' bureau publicity directors. If you're seen as a taker and not a giver, you're going to have a tough time in the future.

When you do get invited, act like a responsible and empathetic adult. Don't be a demanding prima donna. Show up on time. Take notes. Don't get so drunk on free booze that you make a complete ass of yourself and embarrass your host. Be professional. Word gets around quickly if you're not.

# Tax breaks

One of the clear perks of travel writing, if you do it right, is that you get major tax benefits by being able to deduct expenses from your trips. First a disclaimer: I'm no accountant. The tax laws are in constant flux, so consult a professional before acting on any of the deductions advice in this section and don't take my word as gospel.

The general guidelines for deducting business expenses are that there needs to be a clear connection between the expenses and an expectation of making an income from the action of incurring those expenses. The expenses cannot be deducted in pursuit of a hobby.

For many, travel writing *is* a hobby. There is no logical way they will make more in income from their travels than they spend on the travels—ever. The IRS will give you the benefit of the doubt for a time, but after that you need to show a profit. For it to be considered a real business, you are expected to have made a profit in three of the last five years.

This means you could lose a fortune for a couple years, net a few hundred dollars annually the next three years, and you're legit. Keep losing money every year, however, and you are not a professional for tax purposes. Deducting expenses in that kind of situation could invite an audit. The pursuit eventually needs to look like a business and not just something you do for fun.

This is another reason why working for a blogging sweatshop that pays you a small percentage of small revenue does not make you a travel writer, at least in terms of your tax classification. Unless you deduct almost nothing, you can't make enough money to exceed your expenses. Spending $1,000 and writing it off because you made $25 for an article can only work over time if you balance that trip out with others that earned more money. You need to find other ways to create income related to your travels.

There is a workaround though if you think long term. There's no minimum or maximum amount on gains or losses. You can "lose" an unlimited amount in your zero profit years and gain a measly profit in your net positive years. With careful planning and bundling of expenses/income into different calendar years, you can follow the letter of the law and still lose money (bigtime even) for a while.

I did just that when I was first starting out, losing a lot for two years and then showing a profit after that. At first the profit was pretty modest, but now that I make a real income from this I can deduct quite a lot every year. Since I write and edit for so many outlets, there are very few trips I can't deduct as a business expense.

## What you can deduct

Again, get a tax advisor to help with your specifics, but in general you can deduct the following in the U.S. if the expenses were incurred in pursuit of a story you published or tried really hard to publish, assuming your expenses were not covered by a publication hiring you.

- Airline tickets
- Train and bus tickets
- Hotel room charges
- Rental cars and gas
- Mileage for your own car
- Taxi charges
- Admission charges for museums and attractions
- Books and research materials for your story
- Travel magazine subscriptions
- Your internet service
- Seminars and professional dues
- Half your meal expenses while on the road
- Whatever you pay an assistant or intern
- Hosting and domain name charges
- Business equipment and office supplies
- Tax preparation expenses (because you're self-employed)
- Medical insurance and travel insurance

The following are a little dicier, but can be deducted if you can prove you needed them to do your job and you work from home

- Phone service (if you do interviews, phone pitches)
- Cable service (you need some shows/networks for research and ideas)
- Specific software needed for your job
- Massages (if it's a spa story), booze (if it's a cocktail story), or wine (if it's a winery tour story) are all fair game with the right documentation.

As you can imagine, this all quickly adds up to a sizable sum. Even travel writers making good money have little trouble erasing a significant portion of that income through deductions—a positive or negative depending on how you look at it.

Of course if you only go on press trips or on trips where a big magazine is paying your expenses, you won't be laying out a lot of cash. Still though, items like airport transportation, tips to service personnel, and meals while in transit to and from the destination can really add up. Several times I've spent a couple hundred dollars on a "free" press trip because of tips to safari guides or trekking guides.

To make this work, you need to keep meticulous records. Stock up on ink cartridges, jot down all your cash outlays, and save all those scraps of paper—even the handwritten ones in a different language and currency. I've never been audited, but if I ever am it's not going to be a pleasant week for the IRS man. He'll get boxes of receipts from multiple countries in a variety of currencies and he'd better be able to read Spanish.

I sleep well at night knowing that if I ever do get that IRS letter, I'll be ready and able to justify every expense I've claimed. Some push it further than this and will probably get away with it, but I figure the guidelines are fair and generous enough on their own without trying to overdo it. Claim what's defensible and if it feels fishy, it probably is.

Remember too that the goal is to make money, not to create deductions. The advantage of being a travel writer is that every trip has the potential to be another batch of write-offs. If you're not really working on anything related though, it's a vacation, not work. Set yourself up for enough ongoing success financially and your net income will be higher.

I feel like this is one big advantage of being a blogger or running your own site, however. You have far more control over what gets published and paid, so it's easier to justify the expenses as leading to some sort of income. If you have to go pitch an editor for every single possible trip, you don't have as much ammo to defend those expenses.

There's a bit of a gray area in one area though: the idea that you *tried* to get paid for writing about a trip, but gosh darn it, the genius of that big feature idea wasn't recognized by any of the editors you queried. If you can show you sent out repeated query letters and truly tried to get a piece published from your Annapurna Circuit trek, in theory you can write off those expenses. If you were ever audited, that paper trail would be sufficient, but apply some common sense. A new writer who has never earned more than $50 for an article is going to have a hard time proving that a $6,000 trip to Bhutan was really a possible money-making venture. Save that leap for when you're successful.

# Earn While You Sleep

Running an online business of your own is different than writing articles for someone else. The worldwide web is open 24/7, even while you sleep. So you can earn money around the clock.

You have to tend your virtual garden regularly, but the site doesn't care if you're around or not. You can literally make money while you sleep, especially if you have a worldwide audience. There's no feeling like going out for happy hour or a hike and coming back to find you've made more in that time than you did earlier in the day while you were pounding away behind the desk. It's nice to open your dashboard in the morning and find you earned money while you were having happy dreams. This is the real payoff for all that time toiling away for cheap or free in the beginning: real freedom later on.

One interesting byproduct of being a writer in the digital age is that those who own their own content on the web aren't constantly in pitching mode to keep food on the table. If a successful blogger goes on vacation for a week, she still gets paid. If a successful webmaster goes on a two-week vacation in an Italian villa and doesn't add anything new to his resource site, the money will keep flowing anyway.

You can't continue this practice forever, of course: even static resource sites need updating now and then. With blogs you need to "feed the beast" on a regular basis to have fresh content or you start losing readers. Still though, even with blogs you can "future post" by writing things in advance and having then go up while you are away. The point is, you can go on vacation for a week or two completely off the grid and still have some income being generated each day. It's the closest a freelancer gets to a paid vacation.

There have been weeks where I made more money not logging on once than I did being online nonstop in the office. One of the greatest things about publishing on the web is that the earnings are mostly generated by traffic. Readers keep coming to the site whether you are making tweaks or not. Your traffic may dip a little if no new posts are going up, but not by much—at least for a week or two. Sometimes a key media outlet has linked to my blog and traffic has soared while I was hiking or rafting; I was oblivious to the fact my ad revenue had doubled for the week.

# Next Steps to Success

*Always deliver more than you promise, and deliver it on time.*
– Bob Sehlinger, Publisher, Menasha Ridge Press

I can talk for 50 pages about my personal experience and what has worked for me, but everyone comes to the table with different skills and experience. So in this section I will give my advice that will lead to success, but temper it with lots of wisdom from others. I also want to let the editors and publishers tell you what to do since they're the ones who—unless you are purely a successful independent blogger—will be the ones sending you payment for your writing.

In the early part of this book I listed some personal qualities that are important for travel writers. This section is about putting those qualities to work for you, as well as some concrete steps to take in developing yourself as a travel writer.

## Develop a Good Portfolio Site

Before you do anything else on this list, spend the time or money to develop an attractive, professional portfolio site. Make an investment in your future, just as you would by taking a class. Ideally register your domain name at the place where you'll purchase hosting so you don't have to move it later.

I didn't do this right away as soon as I should have, but my dawn-of-the-internet-age website on the old Geocities platform was decent anyway. The one I've had and tweaked since 2005 is great (www.TimLeffel.com). I paid a talented designer in Argentina $250 to set that up for me, then about half that later for a graphics update. It was one of the best investments I ever made. Here are a few more good ones to check out, most of them from people who appear elsewhere in this book:

Joshua Berman – www.joshuaberman.net
Tony Perrottet - www.tonyperrottet.com
Amy Rosen - www.amyrosen.com
Kara Williams - karaswilliams.com
Rory MacLean – www.rorymaclean.com
Darrin DuFord - www.omnivoroustraveler.com
Anja Mutić – www.everthenomad.com

Notice in all but the last two cases the person snagged the domain in their own name, though Joshua Berman had to grab a .net one instead of .com. Really the suffix doesn't matter much: only a few people will automatically put your last name and .com in a browser instead of doing a search. If you have a really common name, you can stick in a middle initial, use a whole different phrase like Darrin or Anja did, or put something like "writer" or "writes" on the end: www.jacobsmithwrites.com.

Try to get some version of your name though and remember that you can put dashes in and achieve the same result. Most search engines treat a dash like a space between words, so tim-leffel.com is just as effective as timleffel.com, for instance. It may even be better if your name is not clear when both are mashed together (like Carollynn or Tomotis).

Do this now. Today! Ideally from wherever you're going to purchase hosting, but if the thought of researching that stresses you out, you can register the domain at Web.com, GoDaddy.com, or wherever and move it later. It will usually cost you $8 to $15 a year depending on the host.

After you've bought the domain name, you can find a good designer by asking around, by using Craigslist, or by using eLance or Sologig. These are sites where freelancers gather to bid on projects. You post what you want (be specific as possible, preferably with examples of what you like) and designers bid on how much they would charge to complete the project. Money goes into escrow and they get paid when the job is complete.

As Sheila Scarborough noted in a blog post she did once, most people—including her—neglect this gateway page because it's a lot of trouble to redesign it and it's not much fun to maintain. "It is a visual wasteland and I'm too cheap to spend any money on it. I'm embarrassed to include the URL on my business cards even though it would be easier for my customers to find me there.." She then asks, "Is your personal website an embarrassing entrance to your online house?"

Giving a terrible first impression is a bad move. This is your billboard, your personal business pitch, and what's almost sure to show up on the first page for searches of your name. If the site is good, this is what you want in the #1 spot. I can't stress enough how important it is to have this site show up first in Google rather than some old article you wrote or your Facebook page. Editors and employers are impatient.

Real grunt work in building something worth showing off isn't always as fun as sending tweets or updating your Facebook page, but those things won't get you many assignments. You also can't control which of them shows up in search engines and where. So get your act together as soon as you have anything to say about yourself and develop a good portfolio page.

Hire a designer if you really want to look professional. But if you're really hurting for money, hunt around for a good template from a hosting company. You can usually get a decent template from the place where you are hosting the site. It won't be as great or as customized as something you invest real money in, but if you pick the right one at least it won't be embarrassing. You will need to learn their interface and probably eventually some basic HTML to tweak the graphics later, but you'll need those skills anyway, so get on it. As I mentioned earlier in the book, you can't beat the deal from iPage.com: $3.50 a month for hosting, a template of your choice, unlimited e-mail (at your domain), and free phone support.

The other option is to build it with the blogging software WordPress, which has lots of advantages (for one thing it's free apart from the hosting), but it takes some work to end up with something looking like a real portfolio page instead of a blog—you need to pick a template that's suited for lots of static pages. Plus WordPress requires regular updates and maintenance.

After it's set up, use that portfolio site as your showcase. You post links to articles on it, a feed from your blog, your LinkedIn page, your Twitter stream, whatever. Just make sure you're linking to things that are professional, not your personal Facebook page filled with baby photos, your dog, and the flower garden in your back yard. This is a business page meant to show you off as a professional, remember?

Don't put this off until you have a big body of list. Get the house done now and then hang your work up on the wall as things get published. If you hate looking at blank spaces, go write some free articles or guest blog posts to get things rolling.

## Write Good Query Letters

As I mentioned earlier, there are entire books devoted to the art of the pitch—writing query letters. When you're starting out, it pays to spend a lot of time on this if you intend to write articles for others as it's the only way you'll get work and the only way you can plead your case.

In its simplest form, a query letter is a short pitch about the idea, information about why you're the person to write it, and why it's right for that particular publication. In cases where the editor doesn't know you and the idea is the main selling point, the first paragraph or two are a taste of your writing and how you would present the material, so typically you would include the lead paragraph from the actual article you plan to submit and then a more explanatory paragraph. Then a paragraph or two on the rest. Sign off and end it.

Edit it to the bare essentials. Many editors won't even read a long query letter. They can tell in a paragraph or two whether it—and you—are worth considering. And they don't have the time or patience to be your grammar coach or writing teacher. So make it great and make the first two paragraphs have what really matters.

---

**Typical Query Letter**

Dear Ms. Editor,

First paragraph that draws the reader in—an approximation of the actual article lede.

Second paragraph with more explanatory info about the story.

Third paragraph about why that publication, where in the publication, and why you're the person to deliver the story.

Any information about timing, photos, and word count.

I look forward to hearing from you soon,

Signature

---

In the days of stamps and letters a query letter was not supposed to be more than one typed page. If anything, editors have even less patience now, so edit it as tightly as possible. For the few newspapers still buying freelance material, the actual query letter isn't very important: those editors want to read the whole story.

Many experienced writers have written a four- or five-paragraph query letter for years. Once you become established, the format above gets superfluous. Once an editor knows you and trusts you, just a simple summary of the idea is enough. One writer I know was flown to the other side of the world to work on a huge feature assignment for a big glossy travel magazine after submitting this query: "I want to go to Yap and I don't know why."

He could get away with that because of his track record. There are a few writers who work for me at Perceptive Travel who don't have to send much more. I know they're talented and will turn even the most mundane destination into an interesting read by pursuing a unique angle. They understand what we want and deliver it.

I tend to lead with my credentials now in freelance queries instead of the story idea for the same reason. First I want the editor to know I'm a pro. Then we can talk about the idea.

What nearly every editor really desires from someone they don't know is this: a writer who gets what their publication is about and either proposes ideas to match or nails assignments that are handed down. Understand the publication well and then pitch something that fits, but something that hasn't been published there before—or at least in the past few years. From the editor's standpoint, if the writer is a proven entity elsewhere, that makes saying yes even easier.

You have to get used to looking into the future too. With magazines, Christmas is in July and summer travel is in January. That's how far ahead they're working on stories. At least ten times now I've gotten a rejection that basically said, "We just did a piece on that." What they are calling "just did" turns out to be an issue that won't hit the stands for two more months, so I couldn't foresee that, but the point is I need to pitch it elsewhere. They've "published" it in house and the editor is looking six months out from now.

Many magazines publish an editorial schedule (often in their "advertise with us" section on the website) and the ones that don't still furnish one to some of the database services mentioned in the resources section at the end. You can study these to get a jump on what they want down the road.

For books, you don't send a query, but a proposal. This is a far more complicated endeavor, so go get a book specific to this subject before diving in so you can do it right. For a book proposal you have to show writing skills, show credentials, show that you have a platform to get the book marketed, and that you have the attitude of a professional.

> *The most common mistake we see are book proposals and manuscripts laden with misspelled words and grammatical and punctuation errors. I also shudder when anyone sends me a book proposal addressed to 'Dear Sir.' Prima-donnas and narcissists are another turn-off. Any author who approaches us demanding special attention, and claiming they deserve to be moved to the head of the line will get rejected"*
>
> – Angela Hoy, Publisher, Booklocker (Booklocker.com)

## Be Original and Creative

There have been many far better trumpet players than Miles Davis. David Gilmour would never win a guitar virtuosity contest. Woody Harrelson will probably never win as many Oscars as Daniel Day Lewis. A lot of people thought Jackson Pollack was a joke as a painter. Jack Kerouac didn't get a lot of respect as a writer at first. Each of these people has or had something going on that intrigued people though. There was a unique creativity evident enough to make people notice.

Too many freelancers make the mistake of spending hours crafting perfectly polished query letters instead of spending hours coming up with original ideas that will make them stand out. If it's been written already, why do you want to write it again? If it's a story or advice column that we can already find on the web, why pitch it to a magazine? As Sean O'Neill of *Budget Travel* says, "Why should you be paid to do what someone else has already provided to a global audience for free?"

In the age of instant Google queries, that means it's harder than ever to be original, but also much easier to make sure your idea is original before you start pitching it or blogging about it. I would argue that O'Neill is being too generous to his editor colleagues—every month I read glossy magazine "list stories" I've read a dozen times before in different forms—but he would probably tell me most of those came out of groupthink staff meetings rather than being pitched by a freelancer.

Even if your publication has a staff of one rather than a conference room of editors, don't retread what others have already done. O'Neill continues, "There's a World Wide Web—link to other sites! And consider following the advice of Jeff Jarvis: 'Do what you do best and link to the rest.' Don't regurgitate what someone else has already written when you can link to that info instead. Focus on providing your own fresh original reporting or insights."

If you want to get noticed, either as a pitching freelancer or a webmaster/blogger creating content that draws readers, originality is key. Sure, in the short term you can draw lots of clicks online with forgettable top-10 lists and steams of posts with "best" or "worst" in the title, but that doesn't build a long-term audience of engaged readers. Editors, publishers, and media people don't call you because you're good at writing linkbait that will get you retweets and hits from Stumbleupon. They want to hire writers with something fresh to say.

Earlier in this book I gave examples of stories that came out of a three-week trip to Peru. I went back again later and covered several other angles. If someone sent me there a third time, I could come up with six or eight more ideas for articles that nobody has ever written before. If I couldn't do that, I'd consider myself a failure as a creative nonfiction writer. If you want to be a successful freelancer—or even a good blogger—finding multiple creative angles is key. Ideas are

> *Content is everywhere. Ask yourself why people should care about what you have to say. It's not 1899 with one weekly new rag. What do you have to say that's different?*
>
> – Sean Keener, CEO, BootsnAll.com

your real currency.

In the magazine world, the writing doesn't happen until you sell the idea. Writing past paragraph number two is pointless if nobody likes the idea to start with. If you're a blogger, who wants to visit your blog to read the umpteenth standard post about visiting the Great Wall of China or staring at the Grand Canyon? Tell us something fresh.

One of the worst rookie mistakes you can make is sending an editor a note that says something like, "I'm going to Paris in June. Could you use any stories from there?" Many aspiring travel writers feel that telling an editor they are heading off to some certain spot on the other side of the globe will result in an enthusiastic invitation to write about it. But here's some news: editors are not short on people who are willing to head off to this place or that to write about it. Don't assume just going somewhere is a reason to write an article. Or even a blog post. Even remote corners of the globe are visited by more writers than we need. Unless you're going to be the first person landing on Mars, you'd better find a good story angle.

This doesn't mean you can't write about popular tourist spots, but you'd better be able to find a truly unique slant that has never been tried before. Wherever you are going, you need to think like a journalist and dig for something an editor will find refreshing—even if that editor is you. Every place I've been to has something interesting going on that nobody is writing about; it just requires researching before you leave, talking to people once you get there, and walking around. Heck, sometimes you can even ask: "What do you wish travel writers

> *My advice? Pack light and think creatively about your story. People want the arc of a story even in the tiniest piece of writing. Writers who are good at teasing a story out of any material are the ones who will make a name for themselves.*
>
> – Zora O'Neill, author and freelance writer

would talk about more for your town/city/resort area?"

Edward Readicker-Henderson went to Hawaii for *Islands* magazine and wrote a feature story about...ukuleles. Darrin DuFord went to New Orleans and wrote about a team that hunts nutria (giant rodents) along the levees. Adam Sachs went to Berlin and wrote about covering three days of expenses for a couple on the same amount the two of them spent for just one meal at a gourmet restaurant on Day One. None of these regurgitated the same tired tourist info about Hawaii, New Orleans, or Berlin.

It is also easier to find a fresh angle, however, if you skip the popular tourist spots altogether. I blew off Prague and biked the greenways of Moravia. My family trip stories have been on cities like Huntsville, Anna Maria Island, and Lexington. The best India story I ever published was about the hash-smoking sadhus in the mountains up north, nowhere near the guidebook sites.

The writers I know that get the most print work are the ones who always find something fresh to say, no matter where they're going. The bloggers who get noticed are the ones doing something original on a regular basis.

## Build relationships

"The key, as is true in any business—especially a highly coveted art form—is to create alliances. Fellow travel writers that I met on press trips proved to be great allies, showing me the ropes, sharing war stories, getting me on to other trips, introducing me to PR companies, and turning me on to media outlets. Relationships. relationships, relationships."

That's the advice from my friend Karen Loftus, who was on a press trip to Iceland with me several years ago. I still keep in touch with her. I've had dinner with two other writers that were on that trip when I visited their city. I've had drinks with another in her city since, and I still exchange e-mails with another writer who was along.

There's a lot of serendipity in being a freelance writer. Tips and assignments can come from odd places you never would have expected. Knowing the right people can make the luck a lot more frequent.

When I've launched new projects and it was time for me to hire writers, half of them ended up being people I knew already. I wasn't an editor when they met me, but I turned out to be one later and I felt best hiring the writers I already knew and trusted. It's an old axiom of business that people find a way to buy from or hire the people that they like. Not the people who are most in their face, mind you, the people that they *like*. So meet people, make friends, find a way to help those people out and someday they might return the favor. That's what makes the world go round.

> *Start following travel writers on Twitter and reading their blogs to find out what they do, what they read, what conferences they attend. Network, network— it's the key to getting "in" with other travel writers who might share contacts, offer you work and give you advice. (Don't expect anyone to hand over their Rolodex to a stranger, but it never ever hurts to befriend others in the field.) If someone buttered me up with, "I admire your work and your career path, do you have any advice for someone starting out," I wouldn't hesitate to recommend some sites where he/she might be able to get some clips.*

– Kara Williams, freelance writer

There are different approaches to this, however, and social media has been both a boom and a bane in this respect. I've got hundreds of Twitter followers than I know absolutely nothing about and I know people who have 1,000 "friends" on their Facebook account, but not many real ones. It doesn't take long to reach a point of diminishing returns with these too-easy tools for networking, especially when you're mixing business and personal contacts together.

How you deal with this is up to you. Some people can juggle 100 contacts and have meaningful relationships with all of them. For others the number may be more like 25. For me, one contact I've met face-to-face or spent a half hour with on the phone trumps nearly all the ones I've never actually talked to except through a software tool.

Whether it's through LinkedIn, the Travel Blog Exchange, MediaBistro, or Twitter, having good contacts (and not just *lots* of contacts) will definitely help your career over time. Go to conferences that make sense if you can. Meet other writers in your city if there's a community there. Spend time on message boards that cater to travel writers. See the resources section for suggestions on all of these.

> *You can't have a 'John Wayne' attitude. You can't do it alone. You need to network so you can learn from other writers and editors. Taking a course taught by a writer for an established travel publication can be very helpful, whether it's an online course by Media Bistro or one offered in-person at a school like NYU. There are too many publications with too many different types of needs for you to be able to make a living pitching all by yourself. Warm up those cold calls to editors by making acquaintances in the industry and by asking pros for career pointers.*
>
> – Sean O'Neill, Senior Editor, Budget Travel

Edward Readicker-Henderson says most of his contacts he has met face-to-face and he credits much of his success to that. "At this point, I'd say the vast majority of work comes from editors I know personally, and I'm just lucky that I know some really powerful editors."

When I asked John DiScala, better known as Johnny Jet, what he would do differently if he had it to do all over again, he said this: "I would network my tail off. Go to travel conferences make friends with people like you, Max from GoNomad, Christopher Elliott, and other well-known personalities and try and write for them for free just to get my name out there."

Don't forget that every contact with an editor is another opportunity to build a long-term relationship. So don't blow it by being unprofessional or telling lies. "Writers forget, or don't know, that I've been a freelancer myself and so I know many of the tricks in the book," says Stuart MacDonald of TravelFish. "If a person can't follow clear instructions—for instance, don't send attachments—what is the chance of them being able to follow more complex editorial instructions? We don't give writers a style guide for the sake of it—they're expected to read and follow it. The good ones deliver what we want, on deadline and generally require very little (if any) editing. Trust is paramount."

If an editor trusts you, that person will give you more assignments, will recommend you to others, and will want to chat with you at cocktail parties. Earn that trust every time and your network will grow.

*Do as much networking as possible, online and offline, getting to know as many people as you can in the industry and building relationships. People who have the ability to hire prefer to hire people they like (assuming everything else is equal), so be sincere and get to know people.*

– Larry Habegger, Executive Editor, Travelers' Tales Publishing

# Persevere, but Be Patient

"Keys to my success? I think perseverance. After being rejected, I stepped back and approached things from another angle. When that didn't work I tried another. Eventually I got my bit of dumb luck and I got 'inside.' I was also lucky that my first book did well enough for my publishers to want to publish another one."

That's from Peter Moore, author of great travel narrative books including *Vroom with a View* and The *Full Montezuma*. He kept at it, still working a day job, after his first book proposal was "promptly rejected by every publisher on the planet." Seven books later he's still making it work and is writing what came out of idea #8.

Chris Epting also has a whole series of books in his biography and makes a comfortable living on royalties, assignments, and speaking engagements. When asked about his success, he says, "The keys have been persistence, tenacity, and follow-through."

To prove that even the most successful writers have moments of doubt, *National Geographic Traveler* Ombudsman (and web entrepreneur) Christopher Elliott says, "I'm not sure if I've broken into travel writing yet! But assuming I have, my key to success is persistence. Never stop!"

Susan Griffith, a freelancer who has penned multiple editions of books on traveling and working abroad says, "So much success in writing is based on luck added to a huge amount of patience."

This is echoed by nearly everyone who looks on paper like an "overnight success." Some will give a nod to dumb luck, a kind editor, or being in the right place at the right time, but it's that ability and willingness to keep at it after repeated rejections and setbacks that separate the winners from the also-rans. Granted you need a modicum of talent, but the most brilliant writers aren't usually the most successful ones. They're too hung up on being artists to keep marketing themselves when it gets hard. Like it or not, successful writers are usually successful salespeople—even if they hate the whole thought that this is what they have to be.

> *I pitch constantly. I don't just send people story ideas (though I do a lot of that, of course). I also seek out companies that are new but highly reputed, or have just gotten a round of funding, or are under-the-radar but publish quality travel editorial. I track down the key editorial contact, and I reach out to them. If I get the slightest encouragement, I continue to follow up for months or years. I hang onto all press releases, save all contacts, and I never forget anything. Also, I don't ever go for one-off story assignments. I want ongoing relationships. I want entire projects, and all the money that goes with them. I like to be on retainer, or on contract.*
>
> - Lena Katz, writer, blogger, and author of three guidebooks on California

David Farley sees it from the writer's side, but also from the teacher's side. "For the last six years I've taught travel writing (at New York University and Gotham Writers' Workshop) and the students who have been the most successful weren't the most talented in the class; they were the most determined and driven. You can always become a better writer through practice and study, but that determination has to come from somewhere else."

## Find your passion and expertise

I've said it many times in many ways in this book: Own your niche and success will follow. The assignments will be easier to come by, you'll eventually get media attention without trying very hard, and you can credibly start your own site or blog that will draw readers in—instead of you having to bust your tail every day to pull people to your site.

Have you ever been on one of those streets of similar restaurants in a tourist town, all jammed together in a block or two, competing head-on? From Peru to Turkey to India I have and for me it's not a pleasant experience. Touts are shouting at me to come into their restaurants, waiters are waving a menu in my face, someone is tugging on my sleeve if I even glance at what's inside the place. If it weren't for the meal deals and the free drinks they often throw in, I'd skip the whole street.

If you start a generalist travel site, that's how aggressive you need to be to make people come eat at your table. As soon as you stop constantly promoting (through friends, through constant social media plugging, through outright begging for links), traffic drops. When you ramp up the hype though, you run the risk of turning people off by seeming like a shameless shill. After a while your pitches are about as welcome as ones from an Amway rep.

What if, however, you're the only pizza restaurant on a street full of seafood shacks? What if you have the only bagel shop in the whole city? You won't please everyone that way, but people will find you on their own and you won't have to drag anyone in against their will.

Figure out what makes you different or better than the thousands of other aspiring writers out there. Discover what aspect of travel gets you the most excited and find a niche that needs filling around that area. Find a fresh place where a hole in the market and your interests can intersect.

Owning your niche is especially important if you're a blogger or author. A study from Cision and George Washington University found that 89% of journalists reported using blogs for their online research. Only corporate websites (96%) are used by more journalists when doing online research for a story. These reporters are seeking out people who know a lot about a specific subject. One of the first things they'll do is a blog search.

Travel writing is increasingly a bad field for generalists. There just aren't many generalist publications out there as newspaper travel sections die off and magazines go on life support. For those at the top of the print pyramid it's still mostly fine, of course, so if you're already there then keep covering the world and all its aspects. If you're just starting out however, you really *really* need to find the path of least resistance. That doesn't mean a coffee specialist can't write about beaches or a diving expert can't write about a wine tour, especially after finding some success, but things will move much faster for you if become known and recognized as an authority in one area.

> *If I had this all to do over again, I'd try to find a genre or specialty, become an expert at it and eventually use the strength of my writing to coast into other realms. I'd exhaustively research the very delicate art of pitching a story. I'd read more. I'd network like mad rather than hiding out in cheapest parts of Eastern and Central Europe. Fortunately, all this things are 10 times more easily accomplished online now than when I was starting out.*
>
> - Leif Pettersen, Lonely Planet author and freelance travel writer

Some manage to stretch this niche a bit and cover several areas well, but usually those areas are complimentary. A writer might focus on luxury resorts, destination weddings, honeymoon spots, and the Caribbean, for example. One trip can result in articles for all those subject areas.

> *With absolutely no experience (or English classes beyond Freshman year of college), I landed a position managing the Personals and Promotions department at a metropolitan alternative weekly newspaper. From there, I started penning a dating advice column, which segued into lifestyle writing. When I made the jump to freelancing full-time in 1998, I had an idea that I wanted to focus on two of my favorite things—food and travel— and so I steered pitches in that direction, and ultimately niched myself as a food, travel and lifestyle writer. I rarely cover any topics that don't fall into that holy editorial trinity.*
>
> - Charyn Pfeuffer, freelance writer

## Find a way to be authentic

We're all drowning in words and communication, but most of it can be—and is—easily ignored.

One of the short cuts to authenticity is writing about what you know well. This can be a certain subject or a place—your home or your adopted home. When I asked freelancer Adam Sachs what he would do differently if he had it to do all over again, this is what he said. "I'd move somewhere. Live somewhere outside of Manhattan for a while. Six months, a year, a decade. I don't think there's any formula for ensuring (or even defining) success but this is just something that can't hurt you as an observer of things."

*Clearly the attention span of the reading audience has greatly diminished as the predominance of print world recedes, just as the symbolic value of experience was lost to some degree when the oral tradition was superseded by the written tradition. Nonetheless, the ever-evolving technological tools provide new ways to convey experiences as a travel writer. Travel writers who succeed while retaining their integrity in the long run read intensely, write constantly, travel frequently, and offer the world another interpretation which is inspirational or practical.*

*Some will succeed in the world of social networking, but it remains to be seen if this is a fad which will produce as much spam as it does the sharing of meaningful information and contacts. I am hopeful that this will be case, and that core human values will not be lost by the constant use of instantaneous and often distracting electronic devices to communicate and live in virtual communities and virtual worlds.*

– Gregory Hubbs, Editor and Publisher, TransitionsAbroad.com

When I asked author Chris Epting if he would do anything differently, he felt he got on the right foot from the start by being original. "Today I think I'd do the same thing I did before when starting out: look for ways to stand out and tell stories that nobody else is telling."

For long articles or blog posts, it's also important to find that elusive thing people talk about but have trouble describing: "voice." When a writer has a voice, the person's prose is unique. Not everyone has this; some people are very successful being chameleons who can adapt to any assignment. If you strive to greatness though, people should be able to recognize your voice in your writing. This is extremely difficult, if not impossible, when writing short pieces for magazines. These get reworked so much by editors that any trace of a voice is gone. With features, blog posts, and books, however, your voice should develop and shine.

> *I don't think success can be ensured by any means. But what I did wrong early on was not try harder. I didn't think bigger magazines would pay any attention to me. Turns out they would. I'd push more to make that jump sooner, spending less time on guidebooks. I would waste less time writing what I thought people wanted, and instead, just spent the time writing my kind of stories. That was a major change for me. When I stopped trying to adapt and just said, "Screw it, this is what I do," my income tripled. Would have been nice to have figured that out sooner.*
>
> – Edward Readicker-Henderson, freelance writer and author

For the most part, voice comes through development and practice, the same way it does for a musician or singer. Over time, that authenticity will shine through.

Authenticity can also be achieved by following good creative nonfiction writing practice. Engage the senses, use lots of examples instead of generalizations, show don't tell, use dialogue from real people (not just cab drivers and bartenders), avoid descriptions we've already heard a hundred times. Describe one incident or scene well instead of trying to cover everything you did on your trip. Remember, most documentaries you see have left out hundreds of hours of footage. Edit just as ruthlessly in your writing.

# Be Professional

If there's one piece of advice that's most important, this is it. For most editors I know, professionalism is a non-negotiable requirement.

Editors don't have the time or patience to deal with writers who don't have their act together. Very few are willing to hold your hand, correct your spelling, soothe your ego, listen to your personal problems that got in the way of completing the assignment on time, or indulge your organizational idiosyncrasies. There are too many other writers out there who are ready and willing to do it right. As Victor Ozols said when I asked him what advice he would give to budding writers, "Make your deadlines. Be one of those people who always meets their deadlines."

This may be a hobby for you, something you do for fun even, but for the people who would pay you, this is a business. Forget that and you're dead before you've started. Most editors will say outright that they'd rather have a competent writer who is dependable than a brilliant writer who is unreliable. Doing what you've promised shouldn't be hard, but it's amazing how many writers blow it in this area.

As Stuart McDonald of TravelFish say, "Obviously writing skill is important, but also an ability to meet deadlines and to not be a time waster. When you're running your own business and relying on freelancers, you don't (or shouldn't) have the spare time to indulge people who don't have the above qualities."

Editors may differ in lots of ways: what kind of queries they like, what kind of writing they prefer, and how formally they define their agreements with writers. If there's one thing that almost all agree on, however, it's that sloppy writers who aren't professional aren't going to get any slack. It's amazing how far you can go by delivering flawless copy submitted on time, every time.

"Flawless" doesn't mean your brilliant prose won't be edited, but it means that you did everything right. You ran a spell check and then had another set of eyes check the text manually. You carefully read the guidelines or style sheet and followed those instructions to the letter. The story is formatted correctly. You double-checked the deadline and got the piece in on time or early. You submitted any additional materials, such as sidebar info or photos, in the manner and format specified by the editor.

**New Writers' Mistakes:**
1) Some do not read the articles on the website.
2) Some do not read the writers' guidelines.
3) Some expect to be paid for any piece they submit, period, while we only accept submissions on spec—except for those who are proven contributors.
4) Some refuse to allow their pieces to be constructively critiqued in order to fit our editorial or the unique requirements for success on the web.
5) Some are closed to learning how to write articles which are of interest to others, and assume that their own experience will be of interest to all. (I believe that those who read all successful forms of media learn to incorporate that intuitively in their writing.)

**Successes:**
1) They have read the best articles on the website and may even want to improve them or offer another perspective.
2) They have read the writers' guidelines.
3) They see gaps in our coverage and offer ideas in detail on how they might approach them.
4) They are open to being edited.
5) They evolve as writers and as travel writers article by article, year by year. They then open up a world of options. The very best continue to experiment and learn.

– Gregory Hubbs, Editor and Publisher, TransitionsAbroad.com

As I was writing this book I got an e-mail from a freelancer asking me for the second time what the deadline was for her article. I replied back with the answer and then reminded her the deadline was in the contract she already had in hand. "Yes, but I filed it away," she replied. "It was easier to just zap you and ask."

*Very* wrong answer!

That writer just got another big X mark on my mental professionalism checklist and that's what will stick with me every time I see a query from her in the future—especially since this was on top of six e-mails sent earlier about the content of the contracted piece. Some of those questions repeated what we had already discussed in earlier e-mails. (Your e-mail program has a search function. Use it!)

An editor is not your psychiatrist, your life coach, your writing instructor, your spell checker, your grammar doctor, your personal Googler, or your travel planner. Some rare ones may befriend you and nurture you if they feel like it, but each one is a *customer* buying something from you in a business-to-business transaction. A customer with very real time constraints and a career-hardened lack of patience for ineptitude.

As Paris-based Karen Fawcett says, "The key to my 'success' was being willing to be there, chase fire engines, generate my own ideas for articles and ALWAYS file on time."

Many editors are more approachable than you would think if you deserve their attention and are a qualified match for their publication. They'll kick around an idea on the phone or discuss what would work best on your upcoming trip across the ocean. All of them are busy, however, so if there's not a clear payoff to your call or e-mails, they don't want to be wasting time. It's always useful to forget about yourself and remember the question that guides the actions of most good sales reps and diplomats: "What's in it for the *other* person?"

What does the person on the other end of the conversation have to gain? Come to them prepared and ready to answer this question, get to the point, and then deliver on your promises if you get an assignment. If you get a no, don't argue. Bow out graciously, thank them for their time, and live to fight another day. Getting the last word may make you feel better, but it's not going to help your long-term prospects.

I have some personal pet peeves as an editor that I know are shared by many others when it comes to professionalism, so here's the inside scoop on how to do things right.

1) Keep your promises and meet your deadlines. You only get one free pass, if that. As Brice Gosnell of Lonely Planet told me, "One writer's aunt has died four times now I think. It was a running joke in the office until we didn't use that writer anymore. One time, okay, but when the same person is late multiple times, they're out."

2) Edit your material well before sending it. Unless we're chatting over a beer somewhere about a potential story idea, I generally don't have time to be your sounding board and angle shaper. Sure, I'll make your article better sometimes through editing, but it should be 95% there before I even get it.

3) Follow the guidelines and the contract. If the style guidelines say, "Third person past tense," don't send an editor an article that's in the first person and present tense. If the agreement you signed says, "2,000 words max" then don't send some 3,500 word novella and give me the chore of chopping it in half. If the guidelines say "American English," don't send a piece with British spellings and cockney slang terms.

4) Don't ever send a query that completely defies the guidelines, thinking your idea is so great that the editor will say, "Oh, forget those silly guidelines." The odds of this succeeding are right up there with the most unpopular boy in high school taking the hottest cheerleader to prom or the local rabbi asking to go to the cathedral with you for midnight mass. If the requirements say something like "Book authors only," "writers with top-tier magazine experience only," or "bloggers who can commit to 10 posts per week," then only query if that requirement applies to you.

> *Not following directions is a common mistake with both old and new freelancers. We list a generic-sounding email address on our acquisitions page for people to use when contacting us. Freelancers think that using connections to get my email address and contact me personally might give them a better chance, but it actually decreases their visibility because I get so much other email. Follow the directions on my site, take my experience requirements seriously, and write a fantastic cover letter that shows a knowledge of our books and how your experience relates to them, and I will notice your resumé—and use it if I have a project that seems like a good fit, even if it's a couple years later.*
>
> - Grace Fujimoto, acquisitions director at Avalon Travel (Moon Handbooks and Dog Lover's Companion series)

## Develop a Good Work Ethic

As I noted at the very beginning of this book, being "on assignment" is often no picnic. It's not uncommon to work all day every day for a week or two straight. Longer if you're a guidebook writer. Here's a Perceptive Travel story excerpt from Rachel Dickinson, who was blogging every day from Ireland for another publication before getting stuck there because of the Iceland ash cloud.

*Everyone had a story. The drunk in the bar. The doorman. The maid from Lithuania. The taxi driver from West Belfast. And I spent my days in a kind of reporter-mode and it was goddamn exhausting. And at night I'd go into my room and try to craft a little story to post. And I'd drink from the bottle of Merlot purchased from the liquor store and eat bread and cheese for dinner bought at the grocery store and I'd begin to feel sorry for myself in this beautiful country of greenness and melodic voices. Then I'd crawl between the 800 thread-count sheets on my perfect bed hoping I'd sleep. I knew I couldn't whine about it lest I get slapped.*

*And each day was the same. Eat breakfast. Look for the story. Plot the trip. Take a white-knuckle drive. Go to another fabulous hotel. Then eat from the grocery store because I couldn't bear to eat out because they don't really get the table-for-one thing in Ireland. No one eats alone. So I started really looking forward to going home.*

Working hard is part of the game for anyone expecting to make real money at this. All the lazy freelance writers you will meet are people who depend on a spouse, a parent, or retirement savings to pay the bills. I'm not saying it's impossible to be a slacker and earn good money as a travel writer, but I have yet to come across someone who is that mythical exception. Read Michael Shapiro's excellent book, *A Sense of Place*, to get a good feel for the writers' life. Even the authors you feel should be able to kick back and take it easy now—Simon Winchester, Bill Bryson, Jan Morris, Rick Steves—still put in full days and then some in front of their computer or doing research on site.

If you work for others, they will expect you to give it your all. If you work for yourself, your readers will expect you to give it your all. Either way, don't choose travel writing because it looks easy. The pros only *make* it look easy on the page.

## Develop a Thick Skin

Doug Lansky seems like the picture of success, with lots of great books under his belt for Rough Guides and Lonely Planet, a column in the *Guardian* newspaper, regular stories in the biggest magazines, and a fun popular website of his own (TitanicAwards.com) that goes with one of his books. It didn't come easy though. "When starting, you'll probably need to 'collect' about 40 rejection letters before you see much progress," he says. "I worked my ass off to get started—12 hours per day for about five months, then I kept working hard after that." But it's important to put all this in perspective. "It was helpful to visit the Rock and Roll Hall of Fame in Cleveland and see all the rejection letters that The Beatles and Rolling Stones received," he adds.

Timothy Ferriss notes the following in his updated version of his runaway bestseller on lifestyle design: "*The 4-hour Workweek* was turned down by 26 of 27 publishers."

As David Farley says, "There's a ton of rejection in this business; know that even the successful writers get rejected frequently." Like most travel writers, I've been rejected by more magazine editors and book publishers than I care to count. It still happens to me on a regular basis now even. I don't keep track; I just bounce off and move on. It's hard not to take it personally, but that gets easier over time as you realize a lot can keep an idea or article from generating a yes with one particular editor. For me, articles that have been dismissed outright by one editor have often gotten picked up elsewhere and then won some kind of "best travel writing" award.

Nobody is perfect, including the managing editor in an office on the 36th floor in Manhattan or the webzine editor working in his pajamas. As much as they hate to admit it, those who do the hiring often make their decisions in a heartbeat, based on emotion as much as the merits of the pitch. If they're in a bad mood or it's the end of the day and happy hour is calling, they may not give your query the attention you think it deserves. What makes it to the "maybe" pile one day may get deleted after a few seconds another day.

Or maybe you made a typo and got immediately dismissed. Or you spelled the editor's name wrong. Or you clearly didn't read the guidelines so your query went straight into the virtual trash bin. Odds are, for a variety of reasons, you will get rejected more often than you get accepted. At first, the ratio may be 100 rejections (or no responses) to one maybe. A year or two later, the ratio should be much better. If not, you're doing something wrong. If you get to a ratio that's better than 10-to-1, you're doing well and if half your pitches get a yes you're a huge success.

Those who don't get rejected are probably getting lazy and are not trying to break into new outlets or get published in a different type of media. It takes a thick skin to be a freelancer, so learn to take rejection (or being ignored) as a routine matter. Learn from it when you can, forge on and keep trying when there's no response to go on. Tweak the idea and try it elsewhere. Pitch that editor with something different. Dive into magazine editorial schedules and find the perfect angle you can pursue locally. Subscribe to a service that will help you figure out what editors are really craving, such as MediaBistro AvantGuild or the Wooden Horse database. And save each rejected idea to revisit later. Use it when you are running your own blog or when you get a regular column where you have creative control.

## Expose Yourself

When you're starting out, your first goal is to get clippings—virtual or physical—and build a portfolio so you've got something to show editors. Even if you're applying for a blogger's spot on a group blog that pays $5 per post, the editor wants to see what you've written already. *Something* at least.

How far should you go to get exposure and build up a portfolio? Should you write for free?

Nothing inspires a more impassioned debate among writers than this subject. If you want to get people fired up on a message board, raise this question and get ready for a flood of responses.

I'll turn down stupid work for free in a heartbeat, but I'm firmly on the side that says, "Write for free when it makes sense for you."

Many writers will point to some free (or close to it) articles they did that gave them something good to build on. There are many other writers who will adamantly tell you that you should *never* write for free. Your skill is valuable and it's an insult to do it for nothing and you bring down the value of the profession and you wouldn't ask your plumber to work for free and yada yada yada. I've heard all the arguments and they're mostly bogus. A plumber is a tradesman and there are barriers to entry for that profession. Anyone can be a writer and at times it seems that half the population is trying to be.

It's not all that hard to string grammatically correct sentences together. Much of the writing out there is "good enough" for what's required. Look at Wikipedia, which is completely written by volunteers. An estimated 10 *million* hours of human labor have gone into Wikipedia alone. One of the most popular travel sites in the world is TripAdvisor, which is completely written with "user-generated content" that didn't earn anyone a cent from their prose.

You can't fight this trend. Whining won't help. This is your competition now if all you can do is express opinions or regurgitate facts about a destination. To earn money from your writing, you need to inspire, inform, or elevate better than the masses can do for themselves.

Remember, nobody owes you a living because you printed up business cards saying you're a writer or you paid for a weekend workshop. To earn money doing this, you truly have to earn it, generally by covering something far better than anyone else.

If you're going to compare professions, compare travel writers to aspiring musicians, actors, songwriters, fashion designers, painters, or sculptors. These people all work for free sometimes until they've really made it. For some they never go beyond that—the passion remains a hobby. Fun jobs with low barriers to entry pay less. That's life. If you don't like it, go to law school so you can earn the big bucks making life more complicated for everyone.

In a story on the Black Eyed Peas that ran in the *Wall Street Journal*, Will.I.Am credited much of the group's success to getting its music out there in any way possible. "Not long ago, the band was lending its music for relatively paltry fees for exposure—a common strategy for emerging acts." This got them onto TV sets via advertising and people started humming their songs. They eventually got a better music deal, real concert sponsorships, and then superstardom. "'It wasn't about the check,' says former manager Seth Friedman.

Exposure opens doors. It gets you in front of an audience, it gets you noticed. It gets links to your portfolio site or blog. Exposure gives you clippings to show editors and it gives you valuable practice. Those who say "exposure doesn't pay" aren't getting exposed in the right place. Or they are bad at marketing and don't know what to do with what they've gotten. Taking gigs that pay little or nothing beats sure beats sending out query after query that goes nowhere.

> *I've learned that this career (like many) comes with a snowball effect. You have to start small, and one thing leads to another. If I were starting all over again, I probably would have reached out to more local publications to build my portfolio before jumping into the game. I've been fortunate to get a lot of great writing jobs, but maybe they would have come sooner if I had a larger portfolio of smaller outlets at the beginning.*
>
> – Ramsey Qubein, freelance writer

For me, exposure has led to mighty things: book deals, article assignments, media coverage, trip invites, and business success. There has been *very* little correlation between article pay scales in the short term and actual long-term monetary benefits. Apart from bragging rights, the biggest magazine assignments haven't done nearly as much for my eventual earnings as a few carefully placed cheap or free articles in the right place have done. It's how you parlay that exposure into something tangible that matters. For example, I used to do a free column that got syndicated by MSNBC. Those stories led to 14 national media interviews and sold a fair number of books from the exposure. The links from them helped my own sites' search engine ranking. The arrangement eventually ran its course, but it was certainly worth the minimal time I put into it repurposing content I already had available.

Starting your own blog is a sure-fire "work for free" proposition in the beginning. My blog didn't make a cent the first two years I ran it except for selling some books. Now it pays my mortgage each month and has gotten me assignments that didn't require a query. The work started out free, but ended up being a pathway to solid income. In the digital world, it's "no pain, no gain."

Free won't pay the bills, of course, so working for little or nothing needs to be a means to an end. Know what you want to get out of it before signing up. The key is doing it when there's a clear payoff. If the site will send major traffic, bring in new blog readers, or raise your site's Google profile with new links, that's worth a lot more in the long run than what some struggling magazine or newspaper will pay you.

For me though, if that eventual payoff isn't worth roughly what I could be making on an hourly basis doing something else, I've got to pass. And if somebody like *Forbes*, AOL, or USAir's magazine asks me to write for free, I'll get as indignant as any writer. Downright insulted actually. If a huge publication with lots of editors on the payroll can't afford to pay the freelancers creating its content, they no longer have a viable and sustainable business. If a major corporation can't pay as much as a one-person blog publisher, they've got a broken business model. That's just exploitation—and bad management.

*Forbes* even had the gall to ask me to contribute a column with no pay, but then said in the same request that I couldn't accept any hosting or press trips. Since when did slave labor come with conditions? Think about how desperate you are for exposure before you fall for an "opportunity" like this just because it comes with a name brand attached. That gleaming name brand may be losing its luster fast in the new media world.

Only you can determine what is worth doing for no pay or low pay. Naturally your standards are going to be lower when you have no experience than they will be later, the same as with a musician or actor. Once you start getting paid work on a regular basis, you can scale back on jobs you've taken just for "exposure," but don't treat that as a dirty word. Nobody gets anywhere in the creative fields without ample exposure, be it an obscure indie film, a community theater part, a free concert in the park, or a travel article that puts a showpiece on that blank slate of writing clips.

## Become a Great Writer

*Write. Write. Write. Then write some more. And if you feel you've had enough, it'd probably be a better idea to do something sensible like becoming a dentist or raising rabbits.*
– Rory MacLean, writer, author, and novelist

If there's one bit of advice that's relatively agreed-upon among the best narrative writers I know—the ones who win prizes and get into book anthologies regularly—it's that being a great "writer" should be the foremost goal, not just being a narrow-casted "travel writer."

> *Forget travel writing. Write. The travel is irrelevant. Stories are what matter, and if you think "travel writing," you doom yourself to a ghetto of mediocrity. Write well. Pay attention. Watch how everything connects, and then write about that. I'm a writer who travels. Write well about the world, about the universals, about the stories that matter to people, and you're way ahead of the game.*
>
> - Edward Readicker-Henderson

Nicholas Gill, whose credits range from *Penthouse* to Frommer's to *Afar* agrees. "Try to be a good writer and a good traveler, but not so much a travel writer. Too many people are infatuated with the title of travel writer, but the best travel books and features are usually written by plain old writers."

There are a few different paths to becoming a great writer, but utilizing all of them can't hurt either.

You can take any kind of creative writing course offered at your local college or participate in workshops held in most cities. Or enroll in a travel writing workshop or course taught by someone who knows the ropes. The best is probably the Book Passage conference held in the San Francisco Bay area each year, but there are others taught by great writers and editors, including some that are featured in the book you are holding now. The best ones allow ample time and occasion to rub shoulders with successful writers and editors and to get your work critiqued. If this is not part of the agenda, the cost should be significantly less.

A less expensive method that many writers feel is equally important is to read a lot. Read a lot of magazines (not just travel mags), read a lot of newspapers or news sites with good international sections (not just the travel section) and read a lot of great books (a mix of travel, novels, and non-fiction). People who do *not* read a lot usually make that obvious in their writing. They use a lot of clichés, they don't use enough dialogue, they don't engage the senses, and they have trouble constructing a sustained narrative. Too often, they come off as a hack who is just in it for the perks. Writers are readers and readers are writers. Build some time into every week to read and as with healthy meals, make sure you're getting a balanced diet.

Almost every experienced writer will tell you to write often as well. Preferably every day, but at least on a very regular basis. As DeliciousBaby.com blogger Debbie Dubrow says, "Writing every day (or almost every day) for my own website was a great way to improve my writing and

> *A lot of people dream of being a travel writer but they don't actually sit down to write. You have to write and read a LOT and have a passion for both. Writing is a craft. It's not something you're born with.*
>
> - Laurie Gough, travel writer and author

develop my voice." This doesn't all have to be writing for publication though. I'd estimate that more than half of us working travel writers got our initial practice keeping a handwritten journal on the road. There's a whole great book on this subject by Lavina Spalding called *Writing Away*. Get it before your next long journey.

If you can get a gig writing for a blog or have the perseverance to run your own, that's great practice. It should be combined with other pursuits since blog posts are only one style, but that's a great place to try out ideas, practice different kinds of writing, and find the kind of focused angles that editors are always looking for. This is often as valuable as a collection of clippings too because the person who would hire you can see how you write on your own, not what your articles look like after intervention by an editor. (Most F.O.B. articles in magazines sound like they were all written by the same person, usually because the editor has had a strong hand in the style and voice, no matter who submitted the initial draft.) Otherwise, get experience any way you can, even if this means writing for free or cheap sometimes or working for low wages on a guidebook for a few months.

Make sure you are getting feedback on that writing though so you know what you're doing well and what needs work. Playing the violin eight hours a day isn't going to make you a better violinist if you have a dozen bad habits and you're tone deaf. I've seen pieces from writers who have written a regular small-town newspaper column for years on end and what they're putting out is still pure drivel. They've not gotten any better at the craft along the way, probably because nobody has called them out on it and the writer has never asked for advice or aimed higher. Keep an eye on your writing and how it is progressing. If you're not seeing an improvement over time and you're not getting better assignments, suck it up and get some help.

> *Only get into travel writing if you really love to travel and write. If you think it's a good pretext for getting to travel, think again: you can travel just as much by saving up money from another, better-paying job, and just taking off to go vagabonding. So only pursue travel writing because you love to write as well.*
>
> - Rolf Potts, travel writer and author

What does it mean to be a "great writer" though and who decides that anyway? You could argue that it's all in the eye of the beholder and like pornography or good art, most editors will say "I know it when I see it." Most books on writing well will at least provide a road map though and give you examples of what makes for compelling writing. Plus if you read a lot, eventually you get a sense of why that feature writer for *National Geographic* got the job or why Bill Bryson got a book contract and you didn't. Sure, some of it's luck and some of it's who you know, but great writers who are persistent usually break through eventually.

For certain styles of publication the basic rules are relatively well-defined. For example:

**Newspapers** want tight sentences, as few adjectives as possible, aggressive avoidance of clichés, AP style (in the U.S.), and lots of service information. In my experience, editors at newspapers are the busiest, the hardest to impress, and the least patient with writers who do not follow directions. The longer the feature the more latitude you get, but wasted words are not appreciated here. You may be required to submit photos with your story, either included in the rate or for a separate fee.

**Magazines** want different things depending on the section. For short articles, they want short sentences that pop and can say a lot without so many words. In my experience, most editors have never met a pun or metaphor they didn't like in these F.O.B. sections. For features, a more narrative, literary style is appropriate, with powerful prose that touches on all the senses and tells a story. Crafting and careful editing are extremely important before you hit that "send" button. Most of all, the editors want something unique and written specifically for them unless it's a custom publication for the likes of AAA, Geico, or RCI, where conventional roundup destination stories are still the norm. For smaller publications, you may be required to submit photos with your story, either included in the rate or for a separate fee. Larger ones will usually hire a professional photographer or use stock photos.

**Websites and Blogs** both want copy that will appeal to search engines. The prose takes a back seat to keyword phrases. So a clever headline and a meandering lede/lead that would work great in a magazine will be a dud for something on the web. The headline and first paragraph need to clearly define what the story or blog post is about. That may appear to be dumbing it down, but reality is that people read differently online, so it's not just for the Googlebots that these elements are simplified. Like it or not, your writing for the web needs to grab a reader within a couple seconds or they're moving on. A good photo or two helps and readers expect links they can follow for more information. Rules can be broken, but in general you need to write in shorter sentences in shorter paragraphs, with more subheads and other elements to break up the text.

**Trade Publications** vary greatly depending on the audience, but in general they are most interested in conveying the facts. Do your homework and write like a reporter. Editors appreciate good writing, but only if it doesn't get in the way of what needs to be conveyed to meeting planners, travel agents, or tour companies. For most trade magazines, revenue comes from regular advertisers and high subscription fees, so positive stories and slants greatly outweigh any negatives about the given industry. You will seldom need to submit photos for these stories as stock photos are commonly used.

**Guidebooks** are clearly meant to guide, so the prime objective is to convey as much useful service information as possible within the pages that are available. What not to include is as important as what to leave in, so writers do not have the luxury of wasted words and meandering sentences. Occasionally you can stretch and show your skills in the sidebars or special sections, but for the most part good guidebook writing means efficient writing. Depending on the publisher, you will often be required to perform other functions, such as sketching out maps or submitting photos of the popular sites. Some require you to shoot photos along the way.

One last bit of advice on writing well: open your horizons across all media. Watch great films with powerful scripts instead of senseless action flicks. Watch great dramas on TV where every word matters instead of ditsy people arguing in interchangeable reality shows. Listen to songs with great lyrics. If Bruce Springsteen, Harlan Howard, or Tom Waits can tell a character's whole story in four minutes, maybe you don't need as many words as you think to make an impact. Take lessons from other media and it will make you a better writer.

## Travel in a Frugal Manner

Travel writers cover lots of nice vacation spots frequented by people with plenty of money, but in reality most of these writers are getting by on the budget of a backpacker.

There are plenty of travel writers out there right now staying in five-star hotels and getting from place to place on a tour bus or with a car and driver. For some publications that works just fine, so many of the big magazines foot the bill for the experience, but for most writers that's a terrible way to travel on a regular basis. Luxury travel is, by nature, sheltering. I love a thick bathrobe and cavernous hot tub as much as the next guy, but not much of a story is going to come out of that unless I'm writing a hotel review.

Putting aside the fact that most travel writers earn well under six figures, luxury travel and good writing don't go together very well. To write good stories you need to take unscripted excursions, talk to new people, eat in restaurants with no tourists, see real local color. You need to leave the TV off and say "no thanks" when a doorman counters your subway question by offering the "special car" service.

The writers who do reputable work that stands the test of time tend to stay in smaller hotels built for mingling. They take public transportation. They eat where the locals eat, preferably in the local market now and then.

The other reason to travel in a frugal manner is that you then have some slim hope of earning a profit from what you are writing. Just one night in a luxury hotel costs more than you would get paid for the average travel article, so unless all expenses are covered by the publication or you're hosted on a press trip—both rare when you're starting out—you want to keep your expenses low. This is why a great number of excellent writers are current or former backpackers, especially bloggers with a big audience. They already know how to wring the maximum experiences out of the minimum expenses. The hack writers who never met a press trip they didn't like, however, are completely lost without a guide and prearranged transportation to take them around. I can usually spot those kinds of writers' stories after reading the first two paragraphs. They're predictable, boring, and don't tell me anything I couldn't have found out myself through a quick Google search.

Sure, those blue bloods doing feature stories for the *New York Times* and *Departures* magazine can afford to stay at the best suites

> *I would encourage anyone who thinks they're cut out to be a travel writer to travel for several months on a restricted budget while maintaining a blog. If they still found the lifestyle attractive, I would then suggest that they start marketing their writing.*
>
> – Beverly Gallagher, freelance writer and blogger

at the best hotels because they don't really need the money. But what comes out on the page is more often than not best perused when you're ready for a nap. As David Mamet said in his book *True and False*, "Where in the wide history of the world do we find art created by the excessively wealthy, powerful, or educated?"

If your entire history of travel is a stream of luxury resorts, air-conditioned deluxe taxis, and cruises, the best thing you could do for your future writing career is to go spend weeks in a cheap country with $1,000, a journal, and a backpack. Your writing will be more interesting and you'll probably have an easier time finding a wealth of angles as well.

Of course there is one way to spend time in a foreign country without eating up all your savings: get a job. One thing Rolf Potts, David Farley, Paige Penland and I all have in common is we each spent more than a year teaching English abroad. Besides this being a great cultural experience, it allows you to have a home base in another country while earning a decent living. Others write while they're on a volunteering mission or are working for the Peace Corps.

As Moon guidebook author Joshua Berman says about travel writing, "Do it and have fun but don't expect it to pay for anything for a while. Find other forms of cheap travel to finance it—like volunteering or studying abroad, or working seasonally in another country."

## But Invest Freely When Needed

A neighbor of mine put his house up for sale more than a year ago and still hasn't sold it. He's a contractor, so it's expertly renovated, impeccably maintained, and he has moved to another house on the same street, so it stays clean and uncluttered. We're in the midst of a housing slump and this particular house is priced a bit higher than the neighborhood norms because it has a pool, but the asking price is not out of whack with comparable sales. So why hasn't it sold yet?

Nobody knows for sure, but it' can't help that the only indication it's for sale is a cheap "For Sale" sign bought at Home Depot, with the owner's phone number scrawled on it with a marker. This guy understands construction and staging, but he obviously doesn't understand marketing. Leaving aside the benefits that a Realtor could provide, what kind of impression does this lousy sign send to potential buyers? How much more attractive would this house be with a professional wooden sign, a good website with lots of photos, and an attractive flyer available to potential buyers driving by?

To me it seems ludicrous to sell a $400,000 house with a crappy looking $10 sign. It's also ludicrous to market yourself as a professional writer if you're not willing to invest any of your own money in development and marketing.

If you struggle to justify buying a $15 book filled with good advice or $55 for an annual AvantGuild membership through MediaBistro, then you lack a basic understanding of the term "return on investment." If you're not willing to spend any of your own money to attend conferences, to travel in pursuit of a great angle— even if it means losing money on the article sometimes—then you're going to need a lot of tremendous amount of luck to make it. You'll constantly be at a disadvantage compared to those who are willing to invest for knowledge and an edge.

Few of us writers can pin our success on one turning point in particular, but there is usually at least a certain period of time when things started getting easier. For me there were several inflection points, all following investments I made in my career that had no guarantee of paying off. I spent six months working on a book, with no guarantee I'd earn anything from it, and even paid for the cover design and P.O.D. set-up fees on my own. I paid a hosting company for a domain name and website at the same time, and then spent another month building the book's resource site. I started a blog without ever dreaming it would become a profit center. I started writing articles that tied into my book with little regard for what kind of payment was attached.

After all that, I got more assignments and the media started calling me for interviews. Then I paid to attend some conferences and networking events. Pitching got easier. Making money got easier.

I later paid a talented designer to build a custom portfolio site to my specifications. Editors started taking me more seriously. I had control of what showed up #1 in Google for my name and it looked impressive.

Later as I branched out into running websites, I paid designers to do it right and I paid freelancers to provide content. I never asked any writer to work for free. I hired assistants to do a lot of the HTML coding grunt work so I could focus on high-value tasks instead. Time after time, I invested real money to create real value.

Most people are, fortunately for me, too timid or too cheap to make all these risky, long-term investments in their future. So it was easy for me to leap ahead of them all and stand out. With a range of different revenue streams, it has been easier for me to weather the storm if something went wrong in one particular area because a recession hit or a country I was covering fell out of favor.

I'm not the only one who has discovered this "success through investment" philosophy though. Most of the webmasters I've profiled in this book have gone down the same path. None of them sat back and waited for the work to come. None of them depended on sweat equity and what they could get for free online to build a business. The old saying, "You've got to spend money to make money," has been abused by some start-ups as a reason to blow through millions of dollars, but at an appropriate level it's true for almost any entrepreneur, freelancer, or solopreneur.

Want to set yourself apart from the pack? Spend constructive money on yourself and your career. Attend conferences now and then. Pay for access to good information. Pay designers to make you look like a pro. Look professional and gain professional knowledge to turn this writing thing into more than a hobby. My experience is only anecdotal, but from what I've seen this willingness to invest in the future is what sets the six-figure travel writers and editors apart from those who struggle to get their earnings past the pocket money level.

## Act Like a Business Owner

According to the 135,000-member Freelancers Union, about 40 percent of their members had trouble getting paid in 2009 and three of four had experienced trouble collecting earned income at some point in their career. Not that self-publishers don't have risk as well, but I'd rather get stiffed for ads that already ran than for an article I slaved over and incurred expenses to research.

As I've said before, being a freelance writer is not an endeavor for the meek. Even if you're a part-timer, treat this like a business. Get promises in writing. Ask for payment terms before taking an assignment. Be persistent about getting paid when the terms have been met.

Figure out how much your time is worth on an hourly or weekly basis and push to make your writing efforts produce that amount in time. Unless this really is no more than a hobby for you, don't treat it like a hobby. Treat it like a business: You, Inc. It's hard to earn like a pro if you don't treat this as a professional business.

## Learn New Skills

Travel Writer 2.0 is not just a writer. To succeed in the future, you will need to be more like a Swiss Army knife than a switchblade that can do one thing only. Continual education and practice in new areas are essential.

*I think this is a very exciting time to be a writer, since we just don't know how the publishing world is going to shake out. I'd say my job has totally changed in the past two years. My job used to be only about the words themselves: having ideas, reporting the story, writing the story, sending it. Now I'm my own photographer and stock agency, I'm dabbling in web design, I'm coding, I would say that learning the basics about photography, web design, and HTML coding are rapidly becoming mission-critical—all of these things that someone else used to handle for us. I'm aware, in doing this, that I'm making myself a far more valuable player in the publishing world. I expect the pay for all this to improve as the economy picks up and advertising dollars return.*

– Alison Stein Wellner

Unless you're regularly appearing in one of the top-tier magazines, it's very hard now to be a writer without also being a photographer. A blog without photos is pretty boring and most web editors expect you to illustrate your own stories. Otherwise they have to go buy photos from a stock agency or hunt down Creative Commons ones on Flickr. So if you're not already a good or great photographer, take a course to learn the basics of framing, lighting, cropping, and creating drama.

There are also books and inexpensive courses out there on basic HTML coding, video editing, and blogging. There are also plenty of free online tutorials if you take the time to hunt around. Invest time, money, or both in making yourself more valuable by being able to do more than string sentences together.

# Enjoy

Travel writing is supposed to be fun. Not as fun as being on vacation, but more fun than being a lettuce picker in the Arizona sun. That's why you want to do it right?

If you look purely at the financial rewards, this is a lousy job. Most travel writers could double their income by taking a corporate job writing RFP responses or software user manuals. We do what we do because we get up in the morning excited about our day. We love the giddy feeling of walking onto an airplane and knowing we'll walk off in a strange new land. We like to wake up in a strange bed and wander through local markets. And although the thrill fades a bit over time, it's exciting to see your name in print—even pixilated print.

So if you're not having fun, return to that "passion and expertise" section. Do not pass Go, do not collect $200. Because you won't collect many dollars if you're not passionate about the subjects or the places you're covering.

Get that part right, then have fun. If you become a success—whatever that means for you—this can be one of the most satisfying and enviable jobs on the planet.

See you on the road!

# Travel Writing 2.0 Resources

As I said in the beginning, this book is meant to be a jumping-off point. Here's where to jump off to when you're ready to develop your skills, find markets for your articles, or start earning money as a blogger or travel website owner.

The most comprehensive set of resources for freelance writers that I've seen is at MediaBistro: www.mediabistro.com/resources/

Sometimes you want something a little *less* comprehensive though, so here's a pared-down list of books and sites that are useful. They may be out of date before the ink is dry though, so keep digging! For a current version of this list that is updated and has links to click, go to www.TravelWriting2.com. (I'm running detailed interviews there as well.)

Ones marked with an asterisk require a fee, but a good paid resource beats a crummy free one any day.

## References and Databases

The following resources and databases commonly list editors to pitch to, their e-mail address, and a phone number for the main desk. A bit of sleuthing will often accomplish the same thing for free (a magazine masthead will have somebody's e-mail address under the business/advertising part you can extrapolate). When time is money though, a database will get you rolling in a hurry.

Your local library (for magazines and reference books)

Writer's Marketplace book – access in the library as the travel section is very sparse

A good newsstand (at Borders or Barnes & Noble you can write down key masthead info and study the issues without buying every one.)

* Scott American Corporation's travel media directory for sale - scottamerican.com
* Wooden Horse media database by subscription - WoodenHorsePub.com
* Mastheads.org subscription service
* TravelWriters.com database access
* Bookmarket.com has downloadable agents and publishers lists
* Publishers Marketplace has databases and a query service at PublishersMarketplace.com

# Job postings and leads

WritersWeekly.com site and newsletter
JournalismJobs.com
Freelanceconnect.com
Press4Travel.com (European)
eLance.com (you pay a portion of revenues)
Sologig.com (you pay a portion of revenues)


* MediaBistro.com Avant Guild service (job postings and some content are free)
* Travelwriters.com (message board and some listings are free)
* WoodenHorsePub.com (free weekly newsletter, but database requires a subscription)
* RealWritingJobs.com (inexpensive trial offered to try it out)
* FlexJobs.com

# Writing , Websites, and Newsletters

Some of these are specific to travel writing, some are for freelancers in general. Many post a steady stream of openings for bloggers and are therefore a better source for online opportunities for beginners than some of the above.

Travel-writers-exchange.com
WriteToTravel.blogspot.com
FabFreelanceWriting.com/blog/
FreelanceWritingGigs.com
MediaJobsDaily - mediabistro.com/mediajobsdaily/
Bookmarket.com – from book marketing expert John Kremer

## *Travel writing sections of travel blogs:*

TransitionsAbroad.com (search for the Travel Writing Portal)
Bravenewtraveler.com/category/travel-writing/ (part of Matador network)
Thetravelersnotebook.com/ (part of Matador network)
WrittenRoad.com (part of BootsnAll)
Rolfpotts.com/writers/index.php (part of Rolf's Vagabonding blog)
Worldhum.com/travel-blog/guide/life-of-a-travel-writer/

## Communities

Travelblogexchange.com – a great community of bloggers trying to find their way and help each other out. Hosts an annual conference.

TravelWriters.com –a bulletin board and posts some market and press trip announcements

Travel-writers-exchange.com/ - message board

MediaBistro's bulletin board - Mediabistro.com/bbs/

MediaKitty.com – a place where PR/marketing people connect with writers for announcements, press trips, and help with assignments.

HelpAReporter.com – THE place where journalists seeking sources post their needs. If you're an expert on something and want media attention, subscribe for free.

## Travel Writing and Creative Non-fiction Courses

There are a million of these out there it seems, but the following survive on results and good word of mouth rather than extreme hype and hard-sell direct mail pitches.

Travel Writing Workshops from Rory MacLean and Dea Birkett - travelworkshops.co.uk
Matador U - matadoru.com/
Paris Creative Writing workshop - Pariswritingworkshop.com
MediaBistro writing courses and webinars- Mediabistro.com/courses/
Writer's Digest courses and webinars – WritersDigest.com
Bookmarket.com has seminars and e-books related to writing, book proposals, and book marketing
Amanda Castleman's courses - Writers.com/castleman.html
Travel Channel Academy - Travelchannelacademy.com (on hiatus at press time, future unknown)
If you live in New York City, check into the Gotham Writer's Workshop. If you are in San Francisco, check into courses run by Larry Habegger.

## Professional Development Associations and Networking Conferences

American Society of Journalists and Authors - asja.org/
North American Travel Journalists Association – natja.org
Society of American Travel Writers – satw.org
Travel Blog Exchange conference – travelblogexchange.com
Book Passage Conference – bookpassage.com
International Food, Wine, & Travel Writers - ifwtwa.com
British Guild of Travel Writers - bgtw.org
Travel Media Association of Canada - travelmedia.ca
Outdoor Writers and Photography Guild - owg.org.uk
Australian Society of Travel Writers - astw.org.au

Writers & Photographers Unlimited - wpu.org.uk

# Good Starting Points for Your Library of Writing Books

(Lonely Planet) *Travel Writing* by Don George (2009)
*Travel Writing: See the World, Tell the Story* by L. Peat O'Neill (2005)
*The Travel Writer's Handbook* by Louise Purwin Zobel and Jacqueline Harmon Butler (2006)
*Writing Away* by Lavinia Spalding (2009)
*A Sense of Place* by Michael Shapiro (2004)
*Do Travel Writers Go to Hell?* by Thomas B. Kohnstamm (2008)
*Smile When You're Lying* by Chuck Thompson (2007)

*Writer's Digest Handbook of Magazine Article Writing* edited by Michelle Ruberg (2004)
*Writer's Digest Guide to Query Letters* by Wendy Burt-Thomas (2009)
*Telling True Stories* by Mark Kramer and Wendy Call
*The Elements of Style* by William Strunk Jr.
*Grammar Girl's Quick & Dirty Tips for Better Writing* by Mignon Fogarty
*ProBlogger* by Darren Rowse and Chris Garrett
*The Well-fed Writer* by Peter Bowerman

# E-books and Reports

Wooden Horse Publishing is a great resource and it's hard to beat the value of what they sell. Their main product is a subscription to their database, which is constantly updated and has key contact information for editors at magazines. They also publish a series of short $5.95 reports by Meg Weaver on specific aspects of freelance writing. Here's a partial list of what was available at press time:

- Calendar Queries: How to Line Up a Steady Stream of Assignments for Next Year.
- Writing Query Letters: Use the Same Proven, Customizable Letter this Veteran Writer Has Successfully Used for Years.
- How to Send 50 Queries per Week.
- Forget the Editors - How to Sell the People Who Really Count.

You can find other good e-books at WritersWeekly.com

## Book Publishers and Agents

If you want to publish a book through the traditional route, find an agent or publisher through one of the following:

*PublishersMarketplace.com
*LiteraryMarketplace.com
*PublishersandAgents.net
AgentQuery.com

Many of the vanity press, print on demand, and e-book publishers are flaky and just out to make money off your set-up fees, but here are a few with transparent terms and reasonable costs. I've only used the first two, however, so do your homework and read all the fine print.

Booklocker.com
GuideGecko.com
Smashwords.com
Fastpencil.com
Lulu.com
Scribd.com

# Featured Travel Writers

A whole bunch of writers contributed their opinions and stories to this book and trusted me with data on their income and earnings mix. I'm incredibly grateful. Here are participating travel writers you should check out when you start looking for role models, books to read, people to follow, or styles to study. They're listed in random order.

**Christopher Elliott** is *National Geographic Traveler* magazine's reader advocate and writes the syndicated Travel Troubleshooter column, which appears in more than 50 U.S. newspapers and Web sites. He produces a popular weekly commentary and podcast on MSNBC.com and writes the Navigator column in Sunday's *Washington Post*. See www.elliott.org.

**Adam Sachs** is a contributing editor for *Travel + Leisure*. He's written about food and travel and other things for *Bon Appetit*, the *New York Times T Style* magazine, *Food & Wine, Departures, Condé Nast Traveler* and many others. Formerly a staff writer for *GQ* and editor of the restaurant section of *Time Out New York*, he was twice nominated for a James Beard Journalism Award. He occasionally updates his blog The Vacationist at adamsachs.org/blog.html.

**Sheila Scarborough** is a writer specializing in travel, tourism, the social web and NHRA drag racing. She's also the co-founder of Tourism Currents, which teaches tourism professionals how to navigate social media. She has print credits but is really a digital communicator, primarily at the following outlets. Family Travel Guide on BootsnAll (familytravellogue.com), Perceptive Travel Blog (perceptivetravel.com/blog), and Sheila's Guide to the Good Stuff (sheilasguide.com) .

**Lara Dunston** is a perpetual globetrotter from Australia who has lived out of her Samsonite since she and her co-author/photographer-

Tim Leffel

husband Terence Carter put their worldly possessions in storage in Dubai (the closest thing they have to a home) in January 2006. Authors of over 40 guidebooks, the couple has bounced around the planet on commissions for Dorling Kindersley, Lonely Planet, Rough Guides, Footprint, AA Guides, Fodor's, Insight and Thomas Cook. In between books, they write and shoot photos for all forms of media, and have done everything from create Paris walking tours for Sony PSP to research Middle East personalities for a series for Lonely Planet TV. Their words and pics have appeared in a long list of magazines and newspapers including *National Geographic Traveler, Wanderlust, The Independent, USA Today*, and *Ritz-Carlton* magazine). Lara reflects upon traveling, why we travel, her work as a travel writer, the media, and the places she and Terry travel to on Cool Travel Guide (cooltravelguide.blogspot.com).

**Bruce Northam** is the writer and host of American Detour and has chronicled tales in more than 100 countries on seven continents. His keynote presentation, Street Anthropology, is a hit on campus and at corporate events and Governor's Conferences on Tourism. His book, *Globetrotter Dogma*, is an award-winning ode to freestyle wandering. Northam is regular contributor to *Long Island Pulse* and Perceptivetravel.com. He's written for *Newsday, National Geographic Traveler, New York Times, New York Post, Details*, and National Public Radio. His other books include *The Frugal Globetrotter* and *In Search of Adventure: A Wild Travel Anthology*.

**David Stanley**—David Stanley is the author of *Moon Handbooks South Pacific, Moon Fiji*, and *Moon Tahiti*, published by Avalon Travel Publishing. His personal website is www.southpacific.org.

**Nicholas Gill** splits his time between Lima, Peru and Brooklyn, New York. He travels across Latin America on a regular basis and his work appears in publications such as the *New York Times, National Geographic Traveler, Condé Nast Traveler, Caribbean Travel & Life, World Hum*, and *Luxury Latin America*. He has also

222

authored numerous travel guides for Frommer's and many other publishers. In 2009, he launched an e-zine on Latin American food, drink, and travel, *New World Review* (www.newworldreview.com). See more at his personal website nicholasgill.com.

**Joshua Berman** is a freelance writer, guidebook author, Spanish teacher, trip leader, location scout, husband, and father. He believes in the philosophy of Outward Bound and the ideals of its founder Kurt Hahn and tries his humble best to employ them in his writing, traveling, and teaching. As a Moon Handbooks author, he specializes in Central America travel, especially in Nicaragua and Belize, and is based in Boulder, Colorado. His biggest trip was a 16-month round-the-world honeymoon, the inspiration for his next book.

**Lan Sluder** is an expert on Belize. The author of a half dozen books on Belize, Sluder has helped thousands of travelers plan a vacation in this fascinating little English-speaking country on the Caribbean Coast of Central America. Among his books are *Living Abroad in Belize; Adapter Kit: Belize, San Pedro Cool; Belize First Guide to Mainland Belize*; *Fodor's Belize* and *Frommer's Best Beach Vacations: Carolinas and Georgia*. Sluder is also founder, editor and publisher of *Belize First Magazine* at belizefirst.com. A former business newspaper editor in New Orleans, where he won a number of New Orleans Press Club awards, Sluder has contributed articles on travel, retirement and business subjects to the *New York Times, Chicago Tribune, Miami Herald, Globe and Mail, Bangkok Post, Newsday*, and *Caribbean Travel & Life*.

**Michael Shapiro** is a travel writer, author, and editor. His feature about Jan Morris' Wales was the cover story of the May/June 2006 issue of *National Geographic Traveler*. Shapiro has recently written about the magic of Kauai for *Islands* magazine and interviewed Studs Terkel for *The Sun*, a literary journal. Shapiro has biked through Cuba for the *Washington Post*, celebrated Holy Week in Guatemala for the *Dallas Morning News*, and floated down the Mekong River on a Laotian cargo barge for an online travel magazine. His work also appears in the *Chicago Tribune, San Francisco Chronicle* and *New York Times*. He's the author of *A Sense of Place: Great Travel Writers Talk About Their Craft, Lives, and Inspiration,* a collection of interviews with famous travel authors. Michael's essay, "The Longest Day" appears in *The Best Travel Writing 2005.* Shapiro contributed the text to *Guatemala: A Journey Through the Land of the Maya* a pictorial book with luminous images by Kraig Lieb, a photographer for Lonely Planet. He teaches annually at the Book Passage travel writers conference near San Francisco.

**Peter Mandel** is a travel journalist and the author of nine books. Mandel has published his articles and essays in *Harper's, Reader's Digest,* and the *Chicago Tribune* and is a regular contributor to the travel sections of the *Washington Post*, the *Boston Globe,* and *National Geographic Kids*. One of his *Boston Globe* articles won the 2005 Lowell Thomas gold award from the Society of American Travel Writers for adventure travel article of the year. Another article, for the *Washington Post,* won a 2006 Lowell Thomas bronze award. Mandel's books have come out from HarperCollins, Penguin, Scholastic, Henry Holt, and Hyperion, among others, and have been featured in *USA Today* and on ABC's *The Home Show*. His titles have been part of exhibits at the Museum of Natural History in New York, at the Smithsonian, and at the National Baseball Hall of Fame, and have been translated into Japanese, Chinese, German, Italian, Dutch, Swedish and Danish.

**Susan Griffith**, a Canadian now based in Cambridge England, specializes in books for travelers who want to work and volunteer abroad. She has written a number of acknowledged classics like *Work Your Way Around the World* (personally updated by her over its fourteen editions), *Gap Years for Grown-ups, Teaching English Abroad* and *Your Gap Year*. More recently she has been contributing travel features to the *Independent*, a UK national daily, on destinations as various as the Swedish Archipelago, Rajasthan, and

Vienna. She is just finishing two regional chapters for a new food-and drink-lover's travel guide to the UK to be called *Taste Britain.*

**Brad Olsen**—Brad Olsen's passion for travel goes far beyond his seven currently published travel books. As a professional writer, artist, photographer, producer, and publisher, Brad Olsen wears many hats and enjoys the challenge. When it comes to extensive world travel, few in the business have the "on the road" experience he has acquired. Brad visited 21 countries in 2004 while researching his new book on sacred sites in Europe. His bi-monthly travel column for *Heartland Healing* magazine "Sacred Destinations: On The Road with Brad Olsen" is currently being considered for syndication. He is also a Contributing Editor for *World Explorer* magazine. Brad Olsen has contributed to several Rough Guides titles, including the *World Party* book. Brad's first book *World Stompers: A Global Travel Manifesto* is now in its fifth edition. His critically acclaimed books in the Sacred Places series include Sacred Places: North America,, Sacred Places Around the World, and Sacred Places Europe. Brad is also the author/illustrator of the Extreme Adventures series of adrenaline-pumping guidebooks. For more see bradolsen.com and cccpublishing.com.

**Chris Epting** is a pop culture history aficionado with a lifelong penchant for documenting the exact sites where things both great and small occurred. What began as an inquisitive hobby soon developed into the writing and photographing of 16 books based on his discoveries, including *James Dean Died Here...The Locations of America's Pop Culture Landmarks, Elvis Presley Passed Here, Even More Locations of America's Pop Culture Landmarks,* then *Roadside Baseball, The Ruby Slippers, Madonna's Bra, Einstein's Brain,* and *Led Zeppelin Crashed Here.* In 2009, *The Early Polo Grounds* and *The Birthplace Book* were released. As an extension of his efforts to chronicle the unique, Epting joins Hampton Hotels for a sixth exciting year as national spokesperson and consultant for the Hidden Landmarks program. Chris is a frequent featured guest on numerous radio and television programs such as National Public

Radio's "All Things Considered," "The Savvy Traveler," "Access Hollywood" and FOX TV's the "Best Damn Sports Show Period." He has contributed articles for such publications as the *Los Angeles Times, Westways, Travel + Leisure* and *Preservation* magazine. One of his stories for Perceptive Travel won a first prize in the Solas Awards and was included in *Best Travel Writing 2009*. For more see chrisepting.com.

**Beverly Gallagher** is based in Costa Rica. She is a freelance contributor to the travel section of the Central American publication, *Tico Times*, a regular contributor to LuxuryLatinAmerica.com, and a freelance hotel reviewer for Northstar Travel Media. She has also published in the Travel & Traditions section of *Fiberarts* magazine and in *San Diego Ranch and Coast*, the city's luxury lifestyle magazine. She is the author of the blog nomadicnarrative.com, which highlights slow and responsible travel and a contemporary nomadic lifestyle, where people live with less to gain more freedom to explore. She originally hails from San Diego, California and has lived on four continents. After teaching English in the United States, Spain and Japan and working in public relations, she decided to combine three of her great loves: writing, language and travel.

**Lena Katz** is the California/Hawaii/Mexico travel blogger for Orbitz, creator of the Playboy Scout news feed, and founding editor of *LAX Magazine*. She is also author of Travel Temptations, a high-end full-color travel guidebook series published on Globe Pequot Press. Frequently quoted as a travel expert in the major media, she is a regular contributor to *Brides* magazine, MSNBC.com, Arthur Frommer *Girlfriend Getaways*, the *LA Times, Forbes Traveler, Robb Report*, Away Networks, *Islands* and other publications. She contributes to a dozen custom pubs including *American Eagle Latitudes, Caesar's Player* and *AAA Going Places*. She was formerly the Los Angeles editor of the multi-million selling *Zagat Restaurant Survey* guidebook. Her commercial writing clients include Sony, MGM/Mandalay, Disney, Gateway, Regent Hotels, and Subaru. See more at lenakatz.com.

**Charyn Pfeuffer** is an adventurous and dependable full-time writer willing to tackle any editorial terrain, but she specializes in food, travel and lifestyle topics. She is partial to Latin American destinations—Chilean cheekbones, Peruvian cuisine, duty free at Jorge Newberry Airport and some kind-hearted Incans have encouraged a fairly regular South of the Equator travel habit. Her extensive credits include *Marie Claire, Imbibe, National Geographic Traveler, Brides,* and *Coastal Living.* See more at CharynPfeuffer.com.

**John DiScala** (a.k.a. Johnny Jet) travels around 150,000 miles and visits over 20 countries each year. He and his website JohnnyJet.com is one of the most popular travel resource sites. It has been featured over 1,800 times in major media publications and he appears regularly on national television as a travel expert. JohnnyJet.com has been named "one of the top best money-saving web sites for travel" by *Budget Travel* magazine, while the *LA Times* calls it "one of the top 10 essential travel resources on the internet." He writes weekly for Frommers.com and he has written for *USA Today, The Boston Herald, LAX Magazine* and *Coast* magazine. See more at JohnnyJet.com.

**Jennifer Miner** is a freelance luxury and travel writer with an extensive background in psychology and counseling, holding two Masters degrees from Columbia University. Born in New York, Jennifer moved from Manhattan to Southern California in 2003. Besides frequent coast-to-coast traveling, she regularly takes work and leisure trips overseas. Reviews of fine dining abroad has grown into a specialty. Traveling often with her two school age children has increased Jennifer's interest in luxury family travel, and sustainable travel. She is one-third of The Vacation Gals bloggers (vacationgals.com), written from the perspectives of three professional travel writers. Jennifer also contributes to Fodor's, Uptake, and AffordableTours. Her posts have been picked up by CNN, Fox Business, Reuters, and the *Chicago Sun Times* and *Palm Beach Post* websites.

Tim Leffel

**Karen Loftus** started out as an award-winning playwright, Tennessee Williams Fellow, and international comedian. After globetrotting through the Middle East, Europe, and Asia, she took a break from touring, slipping into journalism, putting on the page what she once delivered onstage. One surreal year of Hollywood's red carpet later, Karen ran back to the open road in search of more stamps on her passport. As a journalist, Karen naturally found her definitive niche in travel writing, covering vino trends in travel and culinary and cocktail tourism. It was a coming home as her Irish grandparents ran a speakeasy, distilled gin in the tub and ran many a famous pub in Philadelphia. This fashion forward foodie has gone to extreme journalistic measures, parasailing, bungee jumping, four tracking, and canyoning in search of a story. She contributes to a mad mix of outlets and has two travel vlogs of her own: *A Lofty Life* and *Notes From The Road* on Kyte TV (kyte.tv). She is now developing her own wine and spirits based travel show. She is writing a book about her travels and has another book based on her previous comedic travels coming out this year. See more at karenloftus.net.

**Kara Williams** is an award-winning freelance writer who has covered topics ranging from business and babies to skiing and spas in her 19-year editorial career. Kara has been employed as a newspaper reporter, magazine editor and corporate copyeditor. She's freelanced since 1999, and in the past few years travel writing has been the main focus of her work. Her beats include family travel, romantic escapes, girlfriend getaways, spas, outdoor adventures and hotel reviews, with a focus on destinations in North America, Mexico and the Caribbean. Kara's articles have been published in national magazines, regional publications, and local newspapers, as well as online. A social-media junkie, Kara is active on Twitter (@karasw) and blogs regularly at The Vacation Gals (vacationgals.com), which she co-owns with two other professional travel writers. This trio also recently launched the website The Spa Gals (thespagals.com). Kara has spoken about social media and travel blogging at industry events, such as Social Media Strategies for Travel and the Type-A-Mom Conference.

**Peter Moore** is an Aussie travel writer who is the author of six travel narratives: *No Shitting in the Toilet, The Wrong Way Home - London to Sydney the hard way, The Full Montezuma - Around Central America with the Girl Next Door, Swahili for the Broken-Hearted - Cape Town to Cairo by any means possible, Vroom with a View - in search of Italy's Dolce Vita on a '61 Vespa,* and *Vroom by the Sea - the sunny parts of Italy on a bright orange Vespa.* His next book *Blimey! - one man's attempt to become a Brit on the side* will be published in 2010. See more at petermoore.net.

**Jeff Greenwald** was awarded a journalism fellowship by the Rotary International Foundation in 1963 and departed for a second trip to Asia. Over the course of 16 months he lived in Kathmandu, Nepal, and made excursions to the Himalaya, India, Sri Lanka, Hong Kong, Japan, Java, and Bali. His articles about those trips appeared in the magazines *GEO* and *Islands.* It was around this time that he began writing *Mr. Raja's Neighborhood: Letters from Nepal.* Four years later, his travels in Nepal and Tibet would inspire *Shopping for Buddhas,* first published in 1990. A later edition, published in the Lonely Planet "Journeys" series, won the Lowell Thomas Gold Award for Best Travel Book. As he circled the globe writing *The Size of the World* in 1993-1994, Greenwald posted dispatches to the Global Network Navigator, describing his journey. Consequently, he is hailed by several writers as an internet pioneer for creating the first international blog (before the term was coined). In 2003, Jeff Greenwald co-founded the organization Ethical Traveler, of which he serves as the Executive Director. A project of the Earth Island Institute, Ethical Traveler is a global community dedicated to exploring the ambassadorial potential of world travel. Greenwald also developed a one-man show in called *Strange Travel Suggestions.* The show is an improvised monologue whose content is determined by the spin of a on-stage "wheel of fortune." See more at JeffGreenwald.com.

*Tim Leffel*

**Michael Buckley** is a freelance travel writer and photographer based in Vancouver, Canada. He has travelled extensively throughout Southeast Asia, and trekked and mountain-biked in the Himalayan and Karakoram ranges. He is author or co-author of ten books about Asian and Himalayan travel, including *Eccentric Explorers*, a biography-based book about ten wacky adventurers to the Tibetan plateau; *Shangri-La: A Travel Guide to the Himalayan Dream*; a guidebook to Indochina titled *Vietnam, Cambodia and Laos*; *Tibet: the Bradt Travel Guide*, and *Heartlands: Travels in the Tibetan World*. Buckley's feature stories have appeared in dozens of magazines, newspapers and other sources. He is winner of an Indie Excellence Book Award (2009) and a Lowell Thomas Book Award (2003).

**Leif Pettersen** was "Kramered" in 2003 by an unbalanced friend into abandoning an idiot-proof career with the Federal Reserve Bank of Minneapolis and embarking on an odyssey of travel writing. Leif has traveled to 45 countries, living in Spain, Romania and Italy. His work appears in over two dozen books, online publications and magazines, including Lonely Planet guidebooks covering Tuscany, Romania and Moldova. He writes an almost-award-winning, "slightly caustic" blog at KillingBatteries.com, where he dishes on travel writing, Romania, Italian internet, cheap wine, Baby Jebus and his remarkable-gift-for-hyphenation.

**Laurie Gough**, lauded by *Time* magazine as "one of the new generation of intrepid female travel writers," is author of *Kiss the Sunset Pig* and *Kite Strings of the Southern Cross: A Woman's Travel Odyssey*. The latter was shortlisted for the Thomas Cook Travel Book Award, and was silver medal winner of *ForeWord* magazine's Travel Book of the Year in the U.S. Nineteen of her stories have been anthologized in literary travel books. Besides being a regular contributor to *The Globe and Mail*, she has written for the *L.A. Times*, salon.com, the *National Post*, the *Vancouver Sun*, *Canadian Geographic, Outpost*, and the *Daily Express*. For more see lauriegough.com.

**Tom Brosnahan** went to Turkey in 1967 as a Peace Corps Volunteer to teach English. He wrote *Frommer's Turkey on $5 a Day* (1972) as a Peace Corps project. In 1975 he returned to Istanbul on a Fulbright fellowship to study Ottoman history and language, expecting to be a university professor. Instead, he became a travel writer, guidebook author, photographer and consultant on travel information. His 40 guidebooks to a dozen countries for Lonely Planet, Frommer's, Berlitz and Insight have sold over four million copies worldwide, and have been translated into ten languages. Among them are several best-sellers. He has had many articles and photographs published in leading newspapers and magazines, and has served as a founding Contributing Editor for *Arthur Frommer's Budget Travel* magazine. His consulting clients include many top names in the travel and public relations industries, as well as the Turkish Embassy in Washington and the Turkish Ministry of Culture and Tourism. In 2000 he founded Travel Info Exchange, Inc., a developer of destination websites. TurkeyTravelPlanner.com now serves over three million visitors from 213 countries annually. He is also developing the sites NewEnglandTravelPlanner.com and FranceTravelPlanner.com.

**Amy Rosen** is a food and travel writer who writes and illustrates the weekly "Dish" column in the *National Post*, which chronicles her unique culinary experiences across Canada. She is also a contributing editor for *enRoute* magazine. A James Beard nominee, and regular contributor to *Chatelaine* and *Food & Wine* among many other international magazines and newspapers, a story she wrote is included in the anthology *Best Food Writing 2008*. Her long list of writing awards includes multiple wins from three different Perceptive Travel stories and from three different enRoute stories. See more at amyrosen.com.

**Ramsey Qubein** is a travel journalist and full-time correspondent for Northstar Travel Media covering the hotel and airline industry from every corner of the globe. He has traveled to 101 countries (many of them more than two dozen times) and lived in both Madrid and Paris. He has contributed to various consumer and industry outlets including *Business Traveler, Airways*, Singapore Airlines' *Silver Kris*, FoxNews.com, and Next Trip Radio. He serves as the Charlotte Travel Examiner and writes for numerous blogs and web sites in addition to appearing on various broadcast programs. His Master's Degree thesis researched various aspects of branding in the travel industry, and he is highly recognized as an expert in travel loyalty programs, business travel, and the luxury travel segment. He speaks four languages, and, despite flying more than 300,000 miles per year, finds time to make North Carolina his home base.

**Karen Fawcett** has always been able to hop, skip and jump in and out of various different working situations. She has been president and owner of Bonjour Paris (BonjourParis.com) since the site launched more than ten years ago. Prior to that, Bonjour Paris was housed on AOL where Karen derived enormous pleasure from sharing and demystifying "her" France for Francophiles and tourists who were heading to her adopted country. Her first career was as an interior designer. Because of that expertise, she became an ongoing contributor and features writer for *Home Life* magazine and for the lamented *Washington Star* Sunday supplement. After the Star folded, Karen joined many of her colleagues as a contributor at the *Washington Times*. Upon returning to Paris, Karen was able to utilize her journalism background and contributed more than 200 "Expat Abroad" articles to the international edition of *USA Today*. She is accredited by the French Ministry of the Interior as a member of the Foreign Press and was a founding member of the American Institute of Wine and Food's Paris Chapter. She contributes to many other sites including JoeSentMe.com and ConsumerTraveler.com.

**Andy Graham** is the man behind HoboTraveler.com. He became homeless after a six-week Christmas trip to Acapulco, Mexico. While lying in a hammock he realized he never wanted to go home. Confused and excited he returned to the USA, sold all his possessions and took off to visit new friends in other countries. Unknown to Andy at the time, travel is an addiction, after six months he knew he was hooked and after two years, it was hopeless. Twelve years later, he is still perpetually wandering the planet and has chronicled his visits to **88** countries so far.

**John Lamkin** is a freelance travel journalist and photographer who writes on a regular basis for several online magazines, including LuxuryLatinAmerica.com. He is editor of Paloma Blanca Press and an online magazine, Soul of Travel. He is a board member of the International Food, Wine & Travel Writers Association (IFWTWA) where he also serves as Membership Committee Chairman. Although he travels much of the year, mostly in Latin America, he spends his time at home in a small village in northern New Mexico, near Taos or in his second home on a stunningly beautiful lake in southern Mexico. Visit John Lamkin's website at TravelWritingandPhotography.com.

**Lanora Mueller** is a writer-photographer-traveler, dabbler in domestic arts, and mom of teen and adult daughters. She is a blogger and web publisher with a background in marketing communications, electronic publishing, publication design and digital prepress. Based in Chicago, she has lived in France and Britain. See her photography at LanoraMueller.com and her blog at WritingTravel.com.

**Sandra Kennedy** has traveled extensively in thirty-three countries. She taught in American International Schools in Paris, Lisbon and Lima for eight years, but had a dream to combine her travel, photography and writing. After her teaching posts, she began her career as a freelance travel writer and photographer, based in Oregon. Sandra is the author of *Teach and Travel*. Her articles have been published in *International Living*, *The Times* newspaper, *Transitions Abroad*, *40Plus*, *Travel+Leisure UK*, *Oregon* magazine, *Offshore Wave*, and others. She won a first prize in NATJA's annual writing contest in 2009.

**Paige Penland** is an experienced travel writer and guidebook author based in Costa Rica, specializing in Central America and

Southern Mexico. She is the author or co-author of *Great Destinations Costa Rica*, *Great Destinations Oaxaca*, and *Lonely Planet Nicaragua and El Salvador*. See more at PaigePenland.com.

**Beth Whitman** has logged hundreds of thousands of miles around the globe as a contemporary wanderer, combining her love for travel with volunteer work, adventure trips, travel writing, and business. After teaching travel-related workshops in the Seattle area for nearly 15 years, Beth decided to get her message of encouragement and inspiration to more people. She started her own publishing company (Dispatch Travels) and began writing the *Wanderlust and Lipstick* guidebooks for women travelers (now including *The Essential Guide for Women Traveling Solo*, *For Women Traveling to India* and *Traveling with Kids*).

She is the editor of WanderlustAndLipstick.com, the women's travel columnist for Transitions Abroad and occasionally writes for Perceptive Travel. Beth leads trips to India and Bhutan and is toying with leading a group of motorcycle riders through Europe.

**Victor Ozols** is a New York-based writer and editor. His travel writing career began in Riga, Latvia when he worked for an English-language newspaper called *The Baltic Observer*. After moving to New York, he became a contributor for Gridskipper.com, an urban travel blog. From there, he became weekend editor of Jaunted.com, a pop culture travel blog. He was a full time research editor at *Esquire* magazine before moving to *Black Book* and also contributes freelance stories to a variety of other publications. He has a BA in English literature from ODU in Virginia and an MBA in international business from CUNY in New York.

**Gary Arndt** has been traveling and blogging around the world since March 2007. The idea for running a travel blog during his trip didn't come until later, but like the idea of the trip itself, once the idea came, he knew it was something he had to do. He runs (and makes a living from) Everything-everywhere.com, which is one of the most popular travel blogs on the web.

**Rory MacLean** made a cardboard-and-crayon world atlas as a child, slipping imaginary lands between the countries which he knew. His six travel books, including UK best-sellers *Stalin's Nose* and *Under the Dragon*, have challenged and invigorated the genre, and—according to the late John Fowles— are among works that "marvellously explain why literature still lives." He has won the *Yorkshire Post* Best First Work prize and an Arts Council Writers' Award, was twice shortlisted for the Thomas Cook Travel Book Prize and was nominated for the International IMPAC Dublin Literary award. Born in Vancouver, long resident in the UK, he now lives in Berlin where he is writing a travel book on that city. See more at rorymaclean.com.

**David Farley** is the author of *An Irreverent Curiosity: In Search of the Church's Strangest Relic in Italy's Oddest Town* and co-editor of *Travelers' Tales Prague and the Czech Republic: True Stories*. His writing appears in the *New York Times*, the *Washington Post*, *Travel + Leisure, National Geographic Adventure*, Slate.com, and WorldHum.com, among other publications. He teaches writing at New York University.

**Edward Readicker-Henderson** is a frequent contributor to *National Geographic Traveler, Sierra*, and *Art & Antiques*, among dozens of other publications. He's also a contributing editor at *Islands* magazine. Over the years, he has reported from more than 50 countries and every continent. *Best American Travel Writing* honored Edward in 2008 for the Perceptive Travel story, "How the Last White Rhino in Zambia Wins at Strip Passport," and in 2007 for "The Quietest Place on Earth," as well as "Uses for Dirty Underwear." In 2003, the same book noted "Why You're Here Now," and the next year he won a Lowell Thomas Award for the "Under the Protection of the Cow Demon." He's also recipient of a Northern Lights Award, for the best magazine travel story on Canada. U.S. Poet Laureate Rita Dove remarked that his reflective style was "like watching a particularly elegant sleight-of-hand." The compliment was especially apt, since Edward can also juggle five balls and eat fire.

**Zora O'Neill** has been in the kitchen since she was three, and has the bacon-fat burns to prove it. She taught herself to cook while getting my M.A. in Arabic literature. In fact, it was the most useful thing she learned in grad school. Since then, she's catered weddings, worked the line in New York City restaurants, and run an itinerant dinner party called Roving Gastronome and a more settled one called Sunday Night Dinner in Astoria. SND is the subject of a book from Penguin, *Forking Fantastic! Put the Party Back in Dinner Party*, written with Tamara Reynolds. She has also worked as a guidebook author since 2002 and has authored or contributed to more than a dozen titles for Rough Guides, Lonely Planet and Moon. She's a little compulsive about getting the details right, which is why she maintains update blogs, to let readers of the books know what's changed since the book hit the shelves. See more at RovingGastronome.com.

**Rolf Potts** has reported from more than fifty countries for the likes of *National Geographic Traveler*, the *New York Times Magazine*, Slate.com, *Condé Nast Traveler, Outside, The Believer, The Guardian* (U.K.), National Public Radio, and the Travel Channel. A veteran travel columnist for the likes of Salon.com and World Hum, his adventures have taken him across six continents. Potts is perhaps best known for promoting the ethic of independent travel, and his book on the subject, *Vagabonding: An Uncommon Guide to the Art of Long-Term World Travel*, has been through ten printings and translated into several foreign languages. His newest book is *Marco Polo Didn't Go There: Stories and Revelations from One Decade as a Postmodern Travel Writer*. Though he rarely stays in one place for more than a few weeks or months, Potts feels somewhat at home in Bangkok, Cairo, Pusan, New Orleans, and north-central Kansas, where he keeps a small farmhouse on 30 acres near his family. Each July he can be found in France, where he is the summer writer-in-residence at the Paris American Academy.

**Debbie Dubrow** is a mother of three (ages 4, 2 1/2 and 3mo) living in Seattle, WA. Her blog, DeliciousBaby.com, is about traveling with babies, toddlers and kids. It is filled with personal travel stories, family-friendly city guides and lots of tips and advice for traveling with kids. Debbie offers the perspective and real-world advice that only a mom who travels frequently with her kids can offer. She is proud that her stories on unsafe rental car seats spawned two undercover news investigations and significant changes in corporate policy. Debbie has been interviewed by NPR, teaches classes regularly at the Rick Steves Travel Center, and her stories have been featured at ABC News, Consumerist, the Cookie Magazine Blog, Arthur Frommer's blog, MSNBC.com, and more.

**Durant Imboden** is a U.S.-born travel writer, editor, and novelist who has traveled in Europe (and occasionally lived there) since the age of six. He is also the author of *Buying Travel Services on the Internet*, published by McGraw-Hill, and he has written for *Holiday & Travel* in Britain. He produced his first travel-planning website, The Baby Boomer's Venice, in 1996. He covered Venice and Europe at About.com for 4½ years before launching Europeforvisitors.com in 2001.

**Edward Hasbrouck** is author of *The Practical Nomad: How to Travel Around the World.* He is known as an authority on international travel, airfares, and around-the-world travel. He is also a consumer advocate, investigative journalist, blogger, consultant on travel-related human rights and civil liberties issues with the Identity Project, Policy Analyst for the Consumer Travel Alliance, and contributing writer for ConsumerTraveler.com. The winner of a 2003 Lowell Thomas Travel Journalism award for investigative reporting from the Society of American Travel Writers Foundation for his investigative reporting on the privacy of travel records, Hasbrouck has been in the forefront of efforts to protect the freedom to travel, the privacy of travelers, and their right to control how their personal travel records are used by travel companies and government agencies. He has contributed articles on travel and privacy to *Privacy Journal* and Privacy International's *Privacy and Human Rights* yearbook. Hasbrouck's blog (blah) has been recognized and recommended by major national media and he has been quoted or interviewed in dozens of outlets.

**Alison Stein Wellner** lives in Manhattan, where she was born and raised. She's the culinary travel editor for the *New York Times*-owned About.com, and is a featured member of the editorial team at Luxist, owned by AOL. Her work has appeared in *American Archaeology, Business Traveler, BusinessWeek,* the Christian *Science Monitor, Continental, Fast Company, Glamour, Men's Journal, Money, Mother Jones, New York Magazine, Psychology Today, Robb Report, Sierra Magazine, USA Weekend,* the *Washington Post, Yankee, Yoga Journal,* and more. She's been a contributing editor at Inc. magazine, editor-at-large at American Demographics magazine, a *New York Times* Professional Fellow and a National Press Foundation Fellow. Her articles have won awards from the American Society of Journalists and Authors and the American Society of Business Press Editors.

**Doug Lansky** worked the copying machine at Late Night with David Letterman, *Spy* magazine, and the *The New Yorker* during college, then rejected life as a professional intern and hit the road. He spent two and a half years working his way around the planet: picking bananas in Israel, snowmobile guiding in the Alps, selling carpets in Morocco, and hitching on yachts before a car accident in Thailand brought him home. Six months later, Doug was back on the road, but this time as America's youngest nationally syndicated columnist. His weekly "Vagabond" column grew to reach over 10 million readers in 40 major newspapers. Doug has since written a weekly travel column for *The Guardian,* taught journalism at Colorado College, hosted an hour-long travel documentary for the Discovery Channel/Travel Channel and served as the regular world-travel expert on NPR's flagship travel program, Savvy Traveler, for five years. Doug also tours on the lecture circuit and contributes to

Esquire and other publications while serving as travel editor for Scandinavian Airlines in-flight magazine. His books include *Rough Guides First Time Around the World*, Lonely Planet's *Signspotting*, and *The Titanic Awards*.

**Matt Kepnes** is better known as Nomadic Matt from NomadicMatt.com. He is a twenty-something vagabond who has been on the road regularly since 2005. After a trip to Thailand in 2005, he decided to leave the rat race and explore the world so he finished his MBA, quit his job, and, in July 2006, he set out on an adventure around the world. He finances his travels through his website, which is not only a chronicle of his travels but also a way for people to find inspiration, travel tips, destination advice, travel news, and beautiful photos.

# Acknowledgements

First up, thanks to all the writers and editors who were generous with their time and advice. One guy jabbering for 200+ pages on one subject can get old, so thanks to all of you for making this a more interesting and helpful book to read.

Thanks to Jace Freeman, Steven S. Little, and Spencer Spellman for constructive criticism on the initial draft.

Angela and Richard at Booklocker have provided more support through three editions of *The World's Cheapest Destinations* than I've gotten from any traditional publisher that followed, so thanks to them for providing a good book publishing platform that actually makes business sense for all parties.

As usual, my family put up with me working more hours as this book was being written, but hopefully a year of lazy afternoons in slowed-down central Mexico will make up for that.

Lots of editors hired me over the years when that was the only way to make any money as a writer, so thanks to all of them who printed my work—especially those who hired me multiple times!

I wouldn't be able to make it as a travel writer and publisher without all the book buyers, blog subscribers, and readers of my websites who have supported my publications and my advertisers. You've kept me from being a starving artist and have indirectly contributed pocket money to a whole lot of freelancers. Thank you for coming along on the rides.

# Index

CPSIA information can be obtained at www.ICGtesting.com
Printed in the USA
BVOW060549250612

293528BV00001B/30/P